PA
6537
.T45

Thibault
        The mystery of Ovid's
exile

DATE DUE			

8 1 O

THE MYSTERY OF OVID'S EXILE

THE
MYSTERY
OF
OVID'S EXILE

BY JOHN C. THIBAULT

UNIVERSITY OF CALIFORNIA PRESS

BERKELEY AND LOS ANGELES

1964

University of California Press
Berkeley and Los Angeles, California
Cambridge University Press
London, England

BARBARAE

CONIUGI

IUCUNDISSIMAE

PREFACE

So many and so various have become the hypotheses about Ovid's exile that it does not seem amiss to review them at this time. Consequently, the scope of this work is limited to describing the content of these hypotheses and evaluating the relevancy of the evidence adduced and the cogency of the arguments constructed. No pretense is made, therefore, of succeeding where so many have failed, though it is hoped that eventual success in unlocking Ovid's secret may be facilitated by this critical examination.

My debt to Professor R. P. Oliver cannot be sufficiently expressed or repaid. His encouragement, guidance, and consummate scholarship have done much to make possible whatever may be interesting and worthwhile in this book.

I would also like to thank the editors of the Loeb Classical Library for permission to use the English versions from the Loeb volumes of Ovid's works.

J. C. T.

Santa Barbara
September, 1963

CONTENTS

ABBREVIATIONS

USED IN TEXT AND NOTES

A.A.	Ars amatoria
ad Att.	ad Atticum
ad Georg.	ad Georgica
Aen.	Aeneid
Am.	Amores
Ann.	Annales
Ant.	Antony, Mark
Antiq.	Antiquitates
ap.	apud
Apol.	Apologia
Aug.	Augustus
C.	Carmen
Caes.	Caesar, Julius
CAH	Cambridge Ancient History
CJ	The Classical Journal
De Ben.	De Beneficiis
Dial.	Dialogus de oratoribus
Encyc. Brit.	Encyclopedia Britannica
Ep.	Epistulae
Epig.	Epigrammata
Epit. de Caes.	Epitome de Caesaribus
frag.	fragmentum
Gai. Calig.	Gaius Caligula
Hieron.	Hieronymus
Inst.	Institutiones
Juv.	Juvenal
Mac.	Macrobius

Mart.	Martial
Meta.	Metamorphoses
Olymp.	Olympiad
P.	Epistulae ex Ponto
Quaest. nat.	Quaestiones naturales
R.E.	Real-Encyclopädie
Rem. Am.	Remedia amoris
Rhet.	Rhetorica
Sat.	Saturnalia
Silv.	Silvae
Stat.	Statius
Suet.	Suetonius
T.	Tristia
Tac.	Tacitus
TAPA	Transactions of the American Philological Association
Tib.	Tiberius
TLS	Tristium Liber Secundus

INTRODUCTION

The unknown has always proved so great a challenge that wherever uncertainty dwells—on top of Mt. Everest, at the bottom of the Pacific's Challenger Deep, or on the far side of the moon—man will try to ascertain what is there. Such historic mysteries as the identity of the Man in the Iron Mask or what happened to the Diamond Necklace, never fail to stir the indefatigable curiosity of men. This compulsion to know the unknown is the dynamic spirit behind the persistent efforts of scholars to solve a two-thousand-year-old puzzle of literary history—the secret reason why the Emperor Augustus banished the great poet Ovid.

Though Ovid is himself first to warn against the futility of the attempt (T. I, 5. 45–46, 51–52),[1]

> Scire meos casus siquis desiderat omnes,
>   Plus, quam quod fieri res sinit, ille petit.
>
> .   .   .   .
>
> Pars etiam quaedam mecum moriatur oportet,
>   Meque velim possit dissimulante tegi,

his demurrals have utterly failed to dissuade men of letters from trying to penetrate the barrier of guesswork, omissions, and half-truths beyond which lies the whole truth. The difficulties, far from deterring them, have merely spurred their ingenuity to formulate an imposing array of hypotheses based on the regrettably few facts that are available.

If Ovid's own contemporaries had anything to write about

I

the matter, their words have not survived to enlighten us. But later ages have remedied this lack by producing a kaleidoscopic plethora of comment and interpretation. Indeed, few literary problems can lay claim to as much attention. Evidently, so long as the secret exists, the fascination it exerts will continue to encourage scholars to combine the available facts of history with the amorphous and cryptic allusions of Ovid to form a coherent answer to the enigma.

Though the problem's intrinsic interest thus spurs curiosity to speculate about the nature of Ovid's act, we shall not rashly pretend to have succeeded where so many have failed. The purposes of literary history may be served also by delineating the present status of the problem and by offering a conspectus and critical estimate of the hypotheses. The goal of the present work is limited: it is not to determine precisely the nature of Ovid's fault but to provide a comprehensive survey of the question as it developed in the past and as it stands today, in the hope that further progress with this problem may be facilitated.

To do this properly, we must, at the outset of our investigation, make clear that one goal overshadows all others in Ovid's poems from exile—his desire to win either a full pardon from Augustus or, if the emperor were not disposed to be as magnanimous as that, his permission, then, to live in some place more congenial than outlandish and barbarian Tomis. Quite naturally, this attitude forces Ovid into a literary predicament that prevents him from lying about what is well-known to the emperor and severely restricts his ability to reveal the whole truth, since he must, perforce, make much of what is already widely known, while preserving a cautious silence about the secret mistake that ruined him. Furthermore, Ovid estimated the delicacy of his situation well enough to employ a politic and psychologically sound appeal, through slavish protestations of his guilt, to the mercy of the despot who had personally condemned him. By the

same token he deprived himself of the free use of the evidence that might logically have weighed in his favor but
would certainly have earned the emperor's intense displeasure.

It is necessary, thus, to keep in mind that the poetry composed in exile was conditioned and defined by Ovid's peculiar
intentions in writing it and by the harsh circumstances in
which he lived, if we are to make the needed distinctions for
evaluating correctly in Ovid's poems the evidence concerning his secret mistake.

I

The Outcast

THE RELEGATION

The island of Elba (ancient Ilva) lies off the coast of Etruria and guards the entrance to the Gulf of Folonica. Jason the Argonaut reputedly landed at the island's best port, which was therefore called in antiquity *Portus Argous*. Here it was that the Etruscans first exploited a mountain of iron whose abundance impressed Vergil's fancy (*Aen.* X, 173 f.) and which is still Italy's only domestic source of the metal. This is the island on which Napoleon spent the year of his first exile. And it was on this island that Ovid first learned of the personal calamity which was to blight all the rest of his life.

It appears that Ovid, perhaps frightened and wishing to absent himself from Rome, was in Ilva with his life-long friend, M. Aurelius Cotta Maximus, when rumors of Ovid's offense—*culpae . . . mala fama meae* (P. II, 3. 86) [2] —reached the latter, who, not without difficulty, extracted a presumably complete avowal from the poet, who did not at first give him his full confidence (P. II, 3. 87): [3]

> Inter confessum dubie dubieque negantem
> Haerebam. . . .

Ovid tells us, though his statement may be no more than a precaution to protect a friend, that Cotta as a loyal subject felt that the *dolor Caesaris* must, of course, fill his own breast, and that, accordingly, Cotta's ire was at first as great as Augustus'. Whatever truth there may be in this hyperbole, it is clear that Cotta sooner or later came to sympathize deeply with Ovid, offered him every consolation, and evidently hoped that Ovid might be forgiven by Augustus and the whole affair hushed up (P. II, 3. 91–92): [4]

> . . . mea crimina primi
> Erroris veniâ posse latere vides.

Although Cotta remained on Elba when Ovid returned to Italy (for Ovid did not see him again), he thereafter remained constant in his friendship and doubtless rendered the poet every service in his power.

It has sometimes been assumed that what reached Ovid on Elba was the edict of relegation,[5] but there is no direct evidence for this and the assumption is inconsistent with the probable meaning of Ovid's statement to Cotta (P. II, 3. 65–66): [6]

> Ut tamen audita est nostrae tibi cladis origo,
> Diceris erratis ingemuisse meis.

Since *diceris* implies that Ovid was not present, it would seem that the *cladis origo* was the decree of relegation, news of which reached Cotta, probably still on Elba, after Ovid had taken leave of him and returned to Italy.[7] It is likely, therefore, that the *nuntius* whom Ovid's *mala fama* had brought to Elba was a messenger who summoned him to return to Rome to stand trial or receive punishment.

No public proceedings were instituted against Ovid. Supposedly, one of the two charges against him was too general or was outside the scope of existing law and the other was too delicate for public trial.[8] At all events, Ovid makes it clear that he was not condemned by the senate in its judicial capacity (T. II, 131): [9]

> Nec mea decreto damnasti facta senatus,

and that he was not tried publicly; he says explicitly that he did not appear before a court (T. II, 132): [10]

Nec mea selecto iudice iussa fuga est.

The judge was Augustus himself (T. II, 134): [11]

Ultus es offensas, ut decet, ipse tuas.

These three verses would appear to corroborate and to enlarge the existing evidence for criminal procedures at this time. The traditional criminal court of the period was a republican institution, the *iudicium publicum*. Separate courts, each permanent, were assigned for the several categories of serious crimes—murder, bribery, adultery, and the like. But before Ovid could be tried in the special court that had jurisdiction over his crime—whatever it may have been —someone acting merely as a private citizen would have had to obtain official permission from the chairman of that court to lodge a formal accusation against Ovid. This charge would then be delivered in writing to the praetor presiding over the court who, in turn, would enter the charge into the records, upon which the legal machinery would begin to operate.

Both parties to the suit had some right to determine the composition of the jury, numbering thirty or more citizens, selected from a qualified panel of senators, knights, and lesser officials. When the jurors voted, the majority consensus decided the issue. The judge had no vote, his function being to impose the penalty prescribed by law for the particular offense. No appeal seems to have been permitted from the verdict.

It is possible, however, that Ovid might have been tried in another kind of court, the *cognitio extra ordinem,* in which the magistrate had a freer hand and procedural red tape was cut to a minimum. Eventually, this type of court superseded the ordinary criminal court described above. To bring Ovid's case before this new court no private person need have registered a complaint against him. Instead, the decision of the imperially appointed judge was all that was required to initiate legal proceedings. If an accuser appeared, he was regarded merely as an informer who might be rewarded should the defendant be convicted. The judge could mitigate or intensify the legal penalty according to his discretion and estimation of the degree of guilt. In fact, he was free from the rules of procedure and from the statutory penalties that were binding upon the permanent criminal courts.

An exalted tribunal of the same nature as the *cognitio extra ordinem* was the senatorial court with the consuls, it seems, as the judges. Even as early as A.D. 8, according to Ovid's words, his case might have come before this court that appears to have been reserved customarily for defendants who were important by reason of their nobility, power, or wealth. The crime usually had to be a serious one before it could be submitted to the senate's jurisdiction.

The highest court in this category was presided over by the emperor as judge. Ordinarily, he appears to have had councilors who voted, at least *pro forma,* but there is no compelling evidence to show that he would not, on occasion, forego the pleasure of the republican jury processes to take upon himself the whole weight of determining guilt or innocence.

It may be worthwhile to observe that, although a special permanent court existed to try crimes of adultery and another to try cases of *maiestas,* Ovid was not tried by such a court. Nor was he tried by the senatorial court which was also empowered primarily to hear serious crimes. The reason for this was, of course, that he had committed no such crime —no crime at all, in fact. For he had merely seen something, albeit of so delicate a nature, politically or otherwise, that the privacy of Augustus' chambers was required to protect the imperial secret.

That Ovid saw the emperor personally seems virtually certain, for such expressions as *tristibus invectus verbis* (T. II, 133) [12] are more likely to refer to speech than to the

phraseology of a formal edict (which probably contained no
reference to Ovid's secret *error*); the poet was therefore
given some sort of hearing, however summary, and sentenced
by Augustus in person.

When, however, we attempt to determine the nature of
the proceedings and hearing, we are caught in a dilemma by
the paucity of our information. If we knew the secret offense, we might be able to deduce the probable procedure
used by Augustus, and if we knew that procedure, we could
probably determine within limits the *error* charged against
Ovid. But we really know neither, and hypotheses therefore
tend to become circular. If, for example, Ovid, as many
scholars assume, was somehow linked with the sexual immorality of Julia, either directly as an adulterer or indirectly
through having somehow facilitated her adultery with others
(or even by having influenced her with his poems), it could
be shown that he was probably accused of *laesa maiestas,*
for Augustus, according to the testimony of Tacitus (*Ann.*
III, 24) and Dio Cassius (LVIII, 24), went beyond custom
and the scope of even his own laws in so classifying sexual
misconduct with women of his family.[13] But Owen, Fränkel,
and the others who build a case for the charge of *laesa
maiestas* in this manner are really begging the question,[14]
for it is the assumption that Ovid was tried on that charge
that is used, in turn, to lend support to the hypothesis that
he was involved in Julia's misconduct. But even this is uncertain, for we have no reason to doubt Dio's explicit statement (LV, 10) that after the exile of the elder Julia, Augustus was asked to take judicial cognizance of numerous cases
of adultery among the upper classes of Rome, and did act in
some of the more flagrant and recent cases, decreeing severe
punishments. It would seem, therefore, that he had a special
jurisdiction in such matters, presumably under the *Lex Iulia
de adulteriis.*[15]

We are further handicapped by our lack of detailed knowledge concerning the judicial powers of Augustus and the procedures by which he exercised direct jurisdiction. Indeed, under Augustus, imperial powers were ill defined and in a state of flux, for given the pretense that the "republic had been restored," neither Augustus nor those who hoped to preserve as much as possible of republican institutions, can have wished precisely to define powers that it would have been prudent for both parties to leave vague, in the hope that they might later be extended or curtailed. It is also true that there was a gradual accretion of the powers that Augustus openly exercised during his reign. We are therefore in danger of assuming that Augustus acted according to rules and laws that were not clearly defined and set down until later. It is generally believed, however, though partly on the basis of the standard procedure of later times (Tac. *Ann.* XI, 2), that Augustus did conduct formal trials *in camera,* that is, in a room of his palace or villa, but most likely only in serious cases in which persons of high station were involved and it was desirable to avoid publicity. What meager evidence exists comes from Suetonius (*Aug.* 33. 51) and Dio (LVI. 26), who report altogether three incidents which show Augustus himself either conducting a criminal trial independently of the court system or refusing what appears to be a perfectly normal request to exercise his jurisdiction in this manner. The most persuasive proof, however, that Augustus did hear criminal cases in his own person, is the identical practice of Tiberius who adhered almost slavishly to the procedures and policies of his predecessor. No formal charge was required for this procedure and no appeal was allowed.[16] Augustus was either formally empowered, or took it upon himself to act on the basis of any information, however obtained by him.[17] The procedure was presumably that of *anquisitio,* in which a magistrate conducted the entire trial, limited only by the presence of a *contio* of witnesses, who, under the republic, were regarded as affording the ac-

cused some protection, since they could testify on an appeal
as to what had happened at the trial. With Augustus as the
magistrate, of course, the *contio,* if not actually dispensed
with, would have been a mere formality.

Augustus' judicial powers, although doubtless confirmed
by specific statutes with reference to certain kinds of cases,
were all primarily derived from his *imperium* (Dio LIII,
17. 5–6),[18] for under the Republic the power of *iurisdictio,*
although normally exercised only by the praetors, was held
by all magistrates with *imperium.* We may safely assume
that Augustus took jurisdiction over Ovid by virtue of his
imperium, since neither his tribunitial [19] nor his censorial [20]
powers seem to authorize the action taken, and a *judicium
domesticum* seems to be excluded by the fact that the accused could scarcely have been regarded as a member of
Augustus' family.

Now, if Augustus, in Ovid's case, exercised the *jurisdictio*
inherent in his *imperium* (whether or not confirmed by a
statute covering the kind of offense involved), it seems likely
that he, acting as a magistrate in a *cognitio extra ordinem,*
conducted some sort of formal trial. It is therefore generally
assumed—I believe by all who raise this point except those
who believe that the decree of relegation was issued while
Ovid was on Elba—that Ovid was given a private trial before the emperor. But Ovid does not say so—indeed, he
never alludes to witnesses against him, although it might have
been advantageous for him to suggest that at least the socially inferior, if there were such, had depicted his deed,
whatever it was, in colors darker than necessary. And it is
not strictly necessary to suppose that there was a trial of
any kind.

All that we can be sure of, therefore, is that Ovid was
subjected, probably in person, to a severe tongue-lashing
by Augustus (P. II, 7. 56; T. II, 133), was peremptorily
ordered out of Italy by a specified date (T. I, 3. 5–6), and

was commanded to reside thenceforth in Tomis, a small outpost on one of the most distant and inhospitable frontiers of
the empire. His poems were banned (T. III, 1. 59–82; III,
14. 5–18) from the three public libraries at Rome, the first
of which had been built by G. Asinius Pollio, a great patron
of literature, the other two by Augustus.

The sentence was promulgated by an edict addressed
both to Ovid and to the public (T. II, 135; V, 2. 58). By it
Ovid's life was spared (T. II, 127), his property remained
his own (T. IV, 4. 46), and he retained his rights of citizen-
ship (T. IV, 9. 11). But he was sentenced to proceed to
Tomis and to make his home there. Strictly speaking, Ovid
was punished not by exile but by relegation (T. II, 137; V,
11. 21). A pardon was always possible,[21] and Ovid seems
always to have hoped for it. Owen states that edicts lost their
effect upon the death of the issuing emperor, unless they
were confirmed by his successor.[22] It has been argued that
this was the rule, at least as regards edicts bestowing privileges, in the time of Nerva and Trajan, but the evidence is
by no means conclusive.[23] Furthermore, there is no evidence
at all that such a rule was adopted at the death of Augustus
whose position was such that there was no real precedent.[24]
If there was such a rule, Tiberius must have confirmed Ovid's
sentence, for Ovid remained in exile despite all his efforts
to obtain pardon.

THE DATE OF THE RELEGATION

The date of Ovid's relegation can be determined with reasonable accuracy from two points of reckoning—his own age
and the death of Augustus. The emperor died on the nine-
teenth of August, A.D. 14. News of his passing reached Ovid,
at the extreme edge of the empire, a couple of months later
at the soonest. For the poet indicates, doubtless with some

hyperbole, that a round-trip letter required one year to cover the distance (P. IV, 11. 15): [25]

> Dum tua pervenit, dum littera nostra recurrens
>   Tot maria ac terras permeat, annus abit.

At any rate, the tidings came to him during the fifth year of his residence at Tomis, near the mouth of the Danube (P. IV, 6. 5 f.; 15 f.): [26]

> In Scythia nobis quinquennis Olympias acta est:
>   Iam tempus lustri transit in alterius.
>
>   .   .   .   .
>
> Coeperat Augustus deceptae ignoscere culpae:
>   Spem nostram terras deseruitque simul.
> Quale tamen potui, de caelite, Brute, recenti
>   Vestra procul positus carmen in ora dedi.

The time of the year was winter, the sixth he had suffered through in that grim region (P. IV, 13. 38–40): [27]

> "Caesaris imperio restituendus eras."
> Ille quidem dixit: sed me iam, Care, nivali
>   Sexta relegatum bruma sub axe videt.

These passages, then, place Ovid in Moesian Tomis during the winter of A.D. 9–10. Furthermore, when Ovid received the notice of his relegation, the year was already far gone. So he did not begin his journey to the ends of the earth until December (T. I, 11. 3–4): [28]

> Aut haec me, gelido tremerem cum mense Decembri,
>   Scribentem mediis Hadria vidit aquis.

Down the Adriatic he sailed (T. I, 11. 4), then up the Gulf of Corinth to Lechaeum. Crossing the Isthmus, he took ship to Cenchreae and passed up the Aegean to Samothrace, where he stopped off for a time. He left this island on a boat bound for Tempyra in Thrace. For the rest of the way he traveled overland through Thrace to Tomis (T. I, 10).[29]

The journey was long and wearing (T. I, 4; 5. 58 ff.; 11. 13; III, 1. 12, 42), and Ovid, not eager to press on toward his distasteful destination, probably took advantage of any reasonable opportunity for delay. Occasionally, therefore, he received news from Rome at various halting places (T. I, 6. 8; 9. 39). He does not appear to have arrived in Tomis before the autumn of A.D. 9,[30] for in A.D. 15 he writes (P. IV, 10. 1–2): [31]

> Haec mihi Cimmerio bis tertio ducitur aestas
> Litore pellitos inter agenda Getas.

So Ovid's first summer among the natives had to be in the year A.D. 10. And the edict for his relegation must have been issued near the end of the year A.D. 8.

Ovid was born on the twentieth of March, 43 B.C. (T. IV, 10. 13; *Fasti* III, 813). He says that he was fifty years old when the wrath of Augustus reached him on the island of Elba where he was staying (T. IV, 8. 33; 10. 96; P. II, 3). Again this verifies the time of his relegation as the year A.D. 8. Since he was forced to depart hastily, and did so in December, he was not formally exiled much before the end of the year.

THE PERSECUTION OF OVID

When Ovid fell into disgrace, some of his servants and friends naturally found opportunities to plunder or insult him. In the poems written in exile Ovid frequently complains of their perfidy, which astonished him, for his career had theretofore been one of unbroken prosperity. In this group, however, we can distinguish one man, although we cannot identify him by name,[32] who was notable for the ingenuity and the determination with which he sought to despoil and trample on his former friend. His activities are of interest to us since they provide a basis for some speculation concerning Ovid's exile.

Ovid's *Ibis*, written along the same lines as a poem of the same title by Callimachus,[33] although not a translation or adaptation of the now lost Greek model,[34] is an invective directed against an unnamed person [35] who had professed to be Ovid's friend, but who, after Ovid's disgraces made efforts to despoil him of all his property and leave him hopelessly destitute among the barbarians. Although one of the greatest of modern scholars has ingeniously argued that the poem is a literary exercise and that Ovid's enemy is a fictitious character imagined to provide an occasion for the composition,[36] Ovid gives in the beginning of the poem a quite circumstantial account of the persecution of which he was the object. Both verbal parallels and stated circumstances identify this persecution with one specifically mentioned in the *Tristia*. If the beginning of the *Ibis* is poetic fiction and the circumstances to which the poet refers with apparent sincerity are mere invention, we must suspect that the same artifice may have been used in all the poems written in exile.

Ovid says of the man whom he calls Ibis (*Ibis* 11–22): [37]

> Ille relegatum gelidos Aquilonis ad ortus
>   Non sinit exilio delituisse meo;
> Vulneraque inmitis requiem quaerentia vexat,
>   Iactat et in toto nomina nostra foro;
> Perpetuoque mihi sociatam foedere lecti
>   Non patitur vivi funera flere viri.
> Cumque ego quassa meae conplectar membra carinae,
>   Naufragii tabulas pugnat habere mei;
> Et, qui debuerat subitas extinguere flammas,
>   Hic praedam medio raptor ab igne petit.
> Nititur ut profugae desint alimenta senectae:
> Heu! quanto est nostris dignior ipse malis!

Clearly, an attempt was made to take Ovid's property and
this must have been the attempt to which Ovid refers in the
elegy addressed to his wife (T. I, 6. 7–16): [38]

> Tu facis, ut spolium non sim, nec nuder ab illis,
>   Naufragii tabulas qui petiere mei.
>
>   .   .   .   .   ʻ
>
> Aut ut edax vultur corpus circumspicit ecquod
>   Sub nulla positum cernere possit humo,
> Sic mea nescio quis, rebus male fidus acerbis
>   In bona venturus, si paterere, fuit.
> Hunc tua per fortis virtus summovit amicos,
>   Nulla quibus reddi gratia digna potest.

It was made soon after Ovid's departure from Rome, for
the elegy we have last cited, if not written while Ovid was
on his way to Tomis, must have been written shortly after
his arrival there.[39] The *Ibis* may have been written at about
the same time; if, as some scholars suppose, the invective was
written two years later,[40] the enemy persisted in his efforts
to obtain the property, hoping, doubtless, to defeat or out-
maneuver the *fortes amici* who had interceded at the behest
of Ovid's wife. There may be further references to this
malefactor in the other poems written in exile,[41] but if so,
they tell us nothing about the legal basis of the effort to obtain possession of Ovid's property.

Ovid seems to imply that the persecution to which he was
subjected after his departure was somehow connected with
the charge on which he was condemned by Augustus when
he says (*Ibis* 21–24): [42]

> Nititur, ut profugae desint alimenta senectae:
>
> .   .   .   .
>
> Di melius! [sc. fecerunt [43]], quorum longe mihi maximus ille est,
>   Qui nostras inopes noluit esse vias.

Accordingly, those scholars who have discussed the danger
to which Ovid was exposed after his departure from Rome,[44]

have concluded that "Ibis" sought to prosecute Ovid on the
charge of *laesa maiestas*. This assumption, however, involves
a difficulty which appears not to have been taken into account. Whether the primary cause of the condemnation of
Ovid was the *Ars* or the secret *error*, Augustus had pro-
nounced sentence. "Ibis" could, of course, have gone to
Augustus and privately urged him to impose a more rigorous
penalty, but how could "Ibis" have reasonably expected a
reward as delator in a case already adjudicated? If, on the
other hand, "Ibis" planned to bring charges formally in the
courts or before the senate, he could have anticipated the
fashion, under Tiberius, of posing as eager to punish a
heinous offense toward which the emperor, through his ex-
travagant clemency, had been too lenient; but if the charge
which he proposed to bring against Ovid was the *Ars,* it
seems very unlikely that he could have persuaded either court
or senate to increase the penalty; and if the charge was based
on Ovid's *error,* and Ovid is correct in his reiterated implications that Augustus wished the nature of that *error* to be
kept as secret as possible, "Ibis" would have shown a want
of tact inconceivable in a delator. We are therefore reduced
to rather desperate conjectures. Was "Ibis" the man who
originally disclosed Ovid's *error* to Augustus? Ovid says
nothing that would authorize this and implies the contrary;
if *Ibis* 19,

> Et qui debuerat subitas extinguere flammas,

refers to the original anger of Augustus, the statement could
scarcely have been made of an arsonist.[45] Did "Ibis" pretend
to know of aggravating circumstances in Ovid's offense?
The evidence would have had to be submitted privately to
Augustus, and the informer would scarcely be denouncing
Ovid *in toto foro*. Did "Ibis," relying on the instinct of lupine
and human packs to rend the individual who is down, con-
trive some *new* accusation against the disgraced poet? This

would have been no great intellectual feat, for it would have been easy to accuse Ovid of the authorship of some anonymous lampoon or to interpret some passage in the *Metamorphoses* or in an earlier poem as satire covertly directed against the master of Rome. With a court prejudiced by the knowledge that the accused was in disfavor, an adroit delator would have had a fair prospect of success. It is true that Ovid says nothing of such a new charge, but his best reply to it would have been his constant and servile adulation of the despot whom he pretended to regard as a god. If, therefore, "Ibis" was a delator, this conjecture seems to us the most likely explanation of his activity.

Though Ovid's comparison of "Ibis" to a vulture looking for unburied bodies strongly suggests a delator, this is balanced by the affirmation, *debuerat extinguere flammas,* which assumes an obligation that could exist only in the case of a relative or close friend. Such expressions as (*Ibis* 12–13): [46]

> Non sinit exilio delituisse meo;
> Vulneraque inmitis requiem quaerentia vexat

and (*Ibis* 14): [47]

> Iactat et in toto nomina nostra foro

suggest delation of some kind, but Ovid's statement to his wife (T. I, 6. 13–14): [48]

> Sic mea nescio quis, rebus male fidus acerbis
> In bona venturus, si paterere, fuit

as strongly suggests a quasi-legal attempt to occupy property, not a projected accusation which could have led to confiscation. *Fortes amici* (T. I, 6. 15) could, of course, overawe a potential accuser, but their intervention may seem a little more natural, at least in the context suggested to us by the numerous references to such negotiations in the Ciceronian letters, if the title to or possession of property is the point at issue.

All that we can safely conclude, therefore, is that Ovid was, for some time [49] after his disgrace, persecuted by a man whom he had once trusted, and that the poet was in real danger of being reduced to destitution. We should note, however, that neither of the hypotheses we have considered need involve a reopening of the *quaestio* or *anquisitio* which resulted in Ovid's relegation to Tomis.

EFFORTS TO WIN A PARDON

The prospect of passing the rest of his days on the bleak steppes of Moesia amid a rude and alien folk was terrifying to Ovid. Not only was he elderly, delicate of health and grown fastidious in the habits of luxury, but he was, above all, the sort of poet who could flourish only in the drawing-room atmosphere of an ultra-sophisticated aristocracy.

Though the utter reversal of his fortunes prostrated him (T. I, 3. 7–12; 5. 3–6), he began at once to make efforts to procure either remission or at least mitigation of his sentence. To this end, he refused to permit his beloved wife to accompany him into exile (T. I, 2. 41; 3. 81–88),[50] since she was needed at home not only to protect his property and interests, but also to work for his pardon (T. I, 3. 88, 102).[51] Consequently, he instructed her carefully, indicating whom she should approach, and when, and how (P. III, 1. 97–98, 119–122, 147–152). Ovid also solicited the help of his friends and patrons among whom were Paulus Fabius Maximus, the powerful and intimate friend of Augustus (P. IV, 6. 9–16), M. Valerius Messallinus, M. Aurelius Cotta, L. Pomponius Flaccus, Suillius (P. IV, 8), Sextus Pompeius (P. IV, 15. 23), Carus (P. IV, 13), Albinovanus Pedo (P. IV, 10), and Salanus (P. II, 5). These are some of the Romans who, whatever their degree of influence, more or less vigorously and openly made some efforts on behalf of the fallen poet, thus bringing more pressure to bear upon Augustus, in addition to Ovid's direct appeals to him through poetry written in his exile. To Ovid, Augustus seemed at last to be relenting (P. IV, 6. 14), but that gleam of hope was extinguished when the emperor died.

In desperation Ovid appealed, cautiously but vainly, to Tiberius (P. II, 8. 37) and Livia (P. II, 8. 43: III, 1. 97), though he knew that they were not favorably disposed toward him. Germanicus became his last hope for pardon (P. IV, 5. 23–25; 8. 25, 65, 83–86), and in various ways Ovid tried to persuade that popular prince to use his influence on his behalf; for many of Ovid's friends mentioned above were adherents of Germanicus.[52] Not only did Ovid flatter Germanicus in his poetry (P. II, 1), but when Augustus died, he changed the dedication of his unpublished *Fasti* to honor Germanicus instead, and evidently began to substitute his name for Augustus' throughout the poem. He did not, however, complete the revision, and appears in his last days to have despaired, resigning himself to his lot once and for all.[53] Death alone could cancel the edict which had confined him to Tomis, and it was this merciful release that put him beyond the reach of the principate forever, in the year A.D. 18, after nine years of misery among the Getae.[54]

II

Guilty on Two Counts

THE OFFENSE

Quite remarkably, between the time of Ovid's own veiled allusions and the fifth century, we have no mention of the causes of his exile. The silence of four centuries may be in itself significant and it calls, therefore, for brief comment.

We cannot suppose that this silence was merely the result of ignorance. Ovid himself tells us that the real reason for his exile (though not necessarily all of the details) was generally known in Rome (T. IV, 10. 99): [55]

> Causa meae cunctis nimium quoque nota ruinae.

Although *cunctis* is doubtless hyperbolical, there is no reason for doubting the essential truth of the statement. Even the most secret acts of the most efficiently organized and absolute tyrannies seldom escape notice entirely. Considering the conditions in Rome during the Augustan age, we may be certain that even if Ovid had not disclosed the truth to some of his friends, the mystery of his exile could not have baffled the perspicacity and penetration of shrewd observers. At all events, the sudden exile of Rome's most celebrated living poet could not have passed unnoticed and must have given rise to more or less well-informed conjectures as well as a vast amount of gossip.

It is unlikely that the explanations current in Rome were not recorded for the information of posterity. As Dio warns his readers, however, (LIII, 19. 3), the end of the Republic marks the beginning of an official, and therefore mendacious,

historiography, since all official reports issued by a central-
ized form of government are apt to be well-padded with lies.
Furthermore, such lies will be echoed by the pseudo-literary
panderers whose ambition or pusillanimity encourages them
to acquiesce in official deceit. At any rate, the extant works
of Tacitus and Suetonius suffice to prove that information
which the principate wished to suppress, including scandals
affecting the private lives of the rulers, did survive to later
generations, and that much of it, indeed, was recorded in
formal histories which were in general circulation. In the
case of Ovid, however, even the most slavish lackey of the
principate would feel free, if not obliged, to mention at least
the official reason that had been given to explain the relegation of the poet. It may be worthy of note that our earliest
extant source of information, the *Epitome de Caesaribus* that
was annexed to the work of Aurelius Victor, repeats the official story that Ovid was exiled *"quod tres libellos amatoriae
artis conscripsit."* [56]

The silence of four centuries, therefore, must be at least
partly the result of the loss of so much of Roman literature,
including all formal histories of the Augustan age.[57] It is
likely that every extensive account of the period at least repeated the official story. More than this, it may be assumed
that possibly the whole truth was to be found in the *Historiae*
of the elder Seneca and in the *Annales* of A. Cremutius
Cordus, written in a spirit hostile to Augustus and extant
even after they were officially burned in A.D. 25 (Tac. *Ann.*
IV, 35. 4–5), although Quintilian (*Inst.* X, 1. 104) appears
to have known only an expurgated edition. It is also quite
possible that the subject was critically examined in the work
of Aufidius Bassus, and it would be possible to compile a
fairly extensive list of lost works which might have contained
the solution of our problem. In addition to histories and
memoirs, there was at least one certain source of information whose loss must be lamented. The *De poetis* of Suetonius

extended at least to the time of Lucan, so that it almost certainly included a biographical sketch of Ovid, even if the two lines in Jerome, which are generally accepted as coming from that sketch,[58] have another provenance. Ovid would have merited a biography as extensive as that which Suetonius devoted to Horace, and no reader of Suetonius will doubt that he would have told his readers all that he knew about a subject so provocative as the exile of the poet.

Even in the extant writers we seem to have failed to get pertinent information by the merest chance. The younger Seneca, who quotes Ovid so frequently that the latter must have been one of his favorite poets, must have known the full story of Ovid's exile, since his brother was the adopted son of Iunius Gallio, who appears to have been the friend whom Ovid addresses in P. IV, 11. It did not, however, occur to Seneca to allude to Ovid's exile in the *De ira* or in the *De vita beata* which he dedicated to his brother, although Ovid would have been a telling illustration in either context. Statius may have known the full story when he wrote (*Silv.* I, 2. 254):

Nec tristis in ipsis / Naso Tomis,[59]

but the economy of his poem required only a passing allusion to each of the poets whom he enumerates. But it is Tacitus who most cruelly disappoints us if, as is generally believed, he is the author of the *Dialogus de oratoribus*. Tacitus, who makes in the *Annales* an allusion to Ovid's exile that must remain enigmatic for us,[60] introduces in the *Dialogus* laudatory mention of Ovid's *Medea* into the dialogue just before the interlocutor adduces, as another proof of the superiority of poetry over oratory, a contrast between the *inquieta et anxia oratorum vita* and the safe and placid lives of poets. The latter, sheltered from the dangers of political life, enjoy the tranquility and serenity of Vergil, who (*Dial.* 13) "neque apud divum Augustum gratia caruit neque apud populum Romanum notitia." The obvious retort to this speech would have been an observation that Ovid is proof that poets, no less than orators, are in danger of political misfortune. Unfortunately for us, the dialogue is deflected at this point in the speech to the question whether contemporaries are to be compared to writers of the Ciceronian and Augustan ages.

As always, only the most precarious inferences can be drawn from the silence of the extant writers, for there is no context in which failure to mention Ovid's exile would necessarily be significant. The fact that Tacitus says nothing about Ovid when he mentions the return to Rome of the younger Julia's exiled paramour suggests, but does not really prove, that Tacitus did not associate Ovid's misfortune with Julia's disgrace. The silence of Suetonius in his biography of Augustus need mean nothing more than that, as is probable on other grounds and generally believed, he wrote the *De poetis* before the *Caesares*,[61] and saw no reason to repeat himself.

Our only ancient sources of information, therefore, are Ovid's hints, and statements made in or after the fifth century, when both the knowledge of literature and intellectual capacity were rapidly declining.[62]

The task of collecting all of the ancient evidence is not difficult, and a complete review of it will be brief. This evidence will be presented, therefore, in a series of quotations. They will be numbered for later references, placing first all the testimony, however dubious its value (see Chapter XII), from sources other than Ovid which might conceivably be derived from authentic ancient sources, and second, Ovid's own allusions to the causes of his misfortune. The translations for these passages—numbers 1 to 52—will be found in Appendix II.

1. Nam poetam Ovidium, qui et Naso, pro eo quod tres libellos amatoriae artis conscripsit, exsilio damnavit.

An unknown writer *circa* A.D. 400 made this statement in his *Epitome de Caesaribus,* a work erroneously attributed in the MSS. to Aurelius Victor.

2. Et te carmina per libidinosa / Notum, Naso tener, Tomosque missum, / Quondam Caesareae nimis puellae / Ficto nomine subditum Corinnae.

Sidonius Apollinaris, Bishop of Clermont, composed this poem *circa* 450 years after Ovid's death.[63]

3. Pulsum quoque in exsilium, quod Augusti incestum vidisset.

Caelius Rhodiginus, who published his *Antiquae Lectiones* in 1517, included this quotation from Caecilius Minutianus Apuleius, who is thought to have been a grammarian of the tenth or eleventh century.[64]

4. Ipse accusatus fuit apud Caesarem, quia scriptis suis Romanas matronas illicitos amores docuisset.

This is from an *Accessus Ovidii Epistolarum* (III) in the twelfth century Codex Monacensis Lat. 19475.[65]

5. Iste [= Ibis] vero accusarat Ovidium de uxore Augusti, similiter de libro amatorio; quibus causis missus est in exsilium. Alii dicunt quod noluit imperatricem stuprare ab illa rogatus; quae dolens de repulsa accusabat eum apud dominum suum.

Scholium on the *Ibis* in the codex Galeanus of *circa* A.D. 1180 (cf. Ellis, *Ibis,* p. liv); this group of scholia is thought to go back to the sixth or seventh century (*ibid.,* p. lxiii).

6. . . . quo missus erat in exsilium ab Octaviano Caesare propter librum quem scripserat de amore, per quem

The Accessus Ovidii de Ponto, also in the Codex Monacensis, records this.[66]

corrupte fuerant Romanae matronae vel, ut quidam volunt, quia cum uxore sua sive cum puero rem eum habuisse perceperat.

7. Causa triplex est vel propter librum artis quo romanos ad incestum provocaverat . . . Secunda causa est quod dicebatur ab emulis suis quod luderet cum uxore Caesaris . . . Ter***causa fuit quod Caesarem viderat abutentem puero. . . .

This is found in the Codex Guelferbytanus of the twelfth century.[67]

8. Quaeritur autem, cur missus sit in exsilium unde tres dicuntur sententiae: Prima, quod concubuit cum uxore Caesaris Livia nomine. Secunda quod sicut familiaris transiens eius porticum vidit eum cum amasio suo coeuntem . . . Tertia quia librum fecerat de amatoria arte, in quo iuvenes docuerat matronas decipiendo sibi allicere . . .

The passage occurs in an *Accessus* Ovidii Tristium in a twelfth- or thirteenth-century MS, Palatinus Lat. 242, in the Vatican Library.[68]

9. Imperator vero habens eum exosum tum hac de causa [de Arte agitur] tum aliis pluribus de causis, quod concubuisse cum uxore sua dicebatur, et insuper eum facientem quoddam secretum vidit.

The testimony comes from the Codex Barberinus Lat. 26 of the thirteenth century.[69]

10. Scripsit inde epistolas quasdam ad Tiberii filiam sub

The source here is one of the lives of Ovid in the Codex

falso nomine, ac ficto Corinnae inscriptas, quae propter crimen laesae maiestatis
combustae fuerunt. Inde et
exsilium meruit.

Farnesianus of the thir-
teenth and fourteenth centuries.[70]

11.   Postea adamavit Liviam uxorem imperatoris quam falso
nomine apellavit Corinnam,
quasi 'cor urens'. . . .

The source is the Codex
Vaticanus 1479, of the fourteenth century.[71]

12.   Vidit imperatorem Caesarem abutentem puero . . .
et iamque propter uxorem
suam habebat ipsum suspec-
tum et ipsum habebat in
odio propter librum de arte.
. . .

The same Codex Vaticanus
immediately above contains
this declaration, too.[72]

13.   Ovidius occasione libri de
arte praedicti et etiam, quia
imperator eum de uxore sus-
pectum habuit. . . .

A life in the fifteenth-cen-
tury Codex Laurentianus
XXXVI, 18, offers this contribution.[73]

14.   Tres causae exsilii: scilicet
liber de arte, Diana in bal-
neo, Augustus cum puero.

From the Codex Laurenti-
anus XXXVI, 24: Ovid
compares himself to Ac-
taeon, who saw Diana nude.
Some believe he refers to
Livia, or to Julia.[74]

15.   Matronae Romanae nec non
etiam honesti viri eum apud
imperatorem accusaverunt,
illi suae artis vitia obiciendo
et ipsum cum regina vix
adulterium commisisse ad-
dendo.

The statement is contained
in the Codex Laurentianus
XXXVI, 27.[75]

16.   Unde Romanae mulieres
. . . finxerunt, quod ipse
concumberet cum uxore Ne-
ronis.

This is in the fifteenth-cen-
tury Codex Laurentianus
LXXXI, Sup. 23.[76]

17.   Eiciebatur autem in exsilium

The Vatican Palatinus 1707,

propter quaedam carmina. . . .	fifteenth century, offers this conclusion.[77]
18. Tandem cum venisset in suspicionem Augusti, creditus sub nomine Corinnae amasse Iuliam, in exsilium missus est.	The passage comes from a life of Ovid in a codex once owned by Pomponius Laetus, a fifteenth-century scholar. It is extant in the Vatican Library.[78]

Of course, the best testimony about the fault, as well as the bulk of it, comes from Ovid himself. What he says will be found in the following verses from his works.

19. Perdiderint cum me duo crimina, carmen et error. (T. II, 207).[79]	He makes a clear distinction between two factors—one a mistake, the other a poem —that caused his relegation.
20. Utque hoc, sic utinam defendere cetera possem! Scis aliud, quod te laeserit, esse magis (P. III, 3. 71–72; cf. II, 9. 72– 76).	As elsewhere, Ovid indicates that the mistake is the more important of the two causes of his exile.
21. Pars etiam quaedam mecum moriatur oportet, Meque velim possit dissimulante tegi (T. I, 5. 51–52).	In this and other verses he insists that secrecy must cloak the nature of his mistake.
22. Causa meae cunctis nimium quoque nota ruinae Indicio non est testificanda meo (T. IV, 10, 99 f.).	The fault must therefore have been known, at least in general terms, to at least part of Roman society.
23. Ultus es offensas, ut decet, ipse tuas (T. II, 134).	Somehow, the mistake is related to Augustus, whether immediately or remotely.
24. Est mea culpa gravis, sed quae me perdere solum,	But the poet's mistake meant ruin for himself only.

Ausa sit, et nullum maius
adorta nefas (P. II, 2.
15–16).

25. Nec quicquam, quod lege   Yet, whatever the mistake
vetor committere, feci   was, it broke no law of the
(P. II, 9. 71).   land.

26. Quidquid id est, ut non faci- So Ovid never tires of assert-
nus, sic culpa vocanda   ing that no crime was com-
est (P. I, 6. 25).   mitted by him.

27. Non ego caede nocens in   In the same vein, he assures
Ponti litora veni,   King Cotys that he was not
Mixtave sunt nostra dira   guilty of murder, poisoning,
venena manu: or forgery.
Nec mea subiecta convicta
est gemma tabella
Mendacem linis imposuisse
notam (P. II, 9. 67–
70).

28. Causa mea est melior, qui   Nor was he guilty of rebel-
nec contraria dicor   lion.
Arma nec hostiles esse secu-
tus opes (T. II, 51).

29. Non mihi quaerenti pessum-   Ovid had not conspired
dare cuncta petitum   against Augustus.
Caesareum caput est. . . .
(T. III, 5. 45).

30. Non aliquid dixive, elatave   Nor could his mistake be
lingua loquendo est,   laid to careless talk under
Lapsaque sunt nimio verba   any circumstances.
profana mero (T. III,
5. 47–48).

31. . . . sed illo   In any case, his mistake
Praemia peccato nulla petita brought him no advantage.
mihi (T. III, 6. 34).

32. Illa nostra die, quo me   As in #26, Ovid claims al-
malus abstulit error (T.   ways that his action was
II, 109).   only a fault, a mistake.

33. Quod nisi delicti pars ex-   There were mitigating cir-

cusabilis esset (P. I, 7. 41).

cumstances to Ovid's action.

34. Utque hoc, sic utinam defendere cetera possem (P. III, 3. 71)!

But his deed was largely indefensible.

35. Huic ego, quam patior, nil possem demere poenae, Si iudex meriti cogerer esse mei (P. III, 6. 9–10).

Ovid felt obliged to say that he deserved his punishment.

36. Id quoque, quod vivam, munus habere dei (T. I, 1. 20).

In fact, he could have been sentenced to death.

37. Me miserum! potui, si non extrema nocerent,

. . . . .

Ultima me perdunt, imoque sub aequore mergit Incolumem totiens una procella ratem (T. II, 97–100).

Ovid committed his mistake at the end of his successful life. He was destroyed by it in one stroke.

38. Cur aliquid vidi? Cur noxia lumina feci? Cur imprudenti cognita culpa mihi (T. II, 103–104)?

At least three times Ovid emphasizes that his mistake was to have *seen,* inadvertently, a crime.

39. Inscia quod crimen viderunt lumina, plector, Peccatumque oculos est habuisse meum (T. III, 5, 49).

40. Si tanti series sit tibi nota mali (T. IV, 4. 38).

But circumstances led him gradually to this contretemps.

41. Nil nisi non sapiens possum timidusque vocari (P. II, 2. 17).

Stupidity and timidity blinded his judgment, and either allowed him to be carried along to his mistake or prevented him from tak-

		ing prompt action which might have saved him.
42.	. . . sic afuit omne Peccato . . . consiliumque . . . meo (T. IV, 4. 43– 44).	There was no premeditation in what he did.
43.	. . . utque pudore Non caret . . . (T. V, 8. 23).	However, his mistake was such as to cause him to be ashamed.
44.	Et mea non minimum culpa furoris habet (P. II, 3. 46).	He pleads the element of madness to help account for his behavior.

THE POEM

Before we proceed with the investigation of theories about the nature of Ovid's secret mistake, the poem which was the other factor in his relegation has to be considered. The pertinent texts from Ovid will be listed as a preliminary to discussing the possibility that the poem was the sole or principal cause of his ruin.

45.	Ingenio perii Naso poeta meo (T. III, 3. 74).	Often Ovid bewailed his fatal poetic talent, and this line he chose for his tombstone is characteristic.
46.	Sic utinam, quae nil metu-entem tale magistrum Perdidit, in cineros Ars mea versa foret (T. V, 12. 67–68)!	His *Ars amatoria* is the work he blames most often and explicitly for his plight.
47.	Nos quoque iam pridem scripto peccavimus isto: Supplicium patitur non nova culpa novum;	Though Augustus did not like the *Ars amatoria* when the young Ovid published this work, he did not blame

Carminaque edideram, cum   or punish the poet for it
  te delicta notantem   until Ovid had grown old.

.   .   .   .   .

Ergo quae iuvenis mihi non
  nocitura putavi
Scripta   parum   prudens,
  nunc nocuere seni.
Sera redundavit veteris vin-
  dicta libelli,
Distat et a meriti tempore
  poena sui (T. II, 539–
  546).

48. Haec tibi me invisum las-   The charge against Ovid
    civia fecit, ob Artes,   was that his writings under-
    Quis ratus es vetitos solli- mined the institution of
    citare toros.   marriage and taught adul-
    Sed neque me nuptae didi-   tery.
    cerunt furta magistro
    (T. II, 345–347).

49. Quas meruit, poenas iam   For the moment, anyway,
    dedit illud opus (T. I,   Ovid admits that his *Ars*
    I. 68).   deserved its punishment.

50. Ecquid praeterea peccarim,   Ovid sees his poem as a
    quaerere noli,   screen or cloak to conceal
    Ut lateat sola culpa sub   the nature of his mistake.
    Arte mea (P. II, 9. 75–
    76).

51. Vos estis nostrae maxima   Ovid appears to contradict
    causa fugae (T. V, 12.   what he says in #20 by
    46).   claiming here that the
                                 Muses are the principal
                                 cause of his exile, unless,
                                 perchance, his secret error
                                 could somehow be attrib-
                                 uted to the Muses.

The riddle of the relationship between the poem and the
mistake and their comparative importance in bringing about

his relegation is not made easier when Ovid writes (T. IV, 1. 25–26):

> 52.   Scilicet hoc ipso nunc aequa, quod obfuit ante,
>   Cum mecum juncti criminis acta rea est.

Appel believes that this means that the *Ars amatoria* had as much weight as Ovid's error in the charge brought against him. In other words, he believes that because Ovid's mistake was charged to him as a crime, his *Ars* was classified as a parallel and equal offense.[80] De Jonghe thinks that these lines should be understood to mean only that the *Ars* shared the guilt of a wrong which was connected with Ovid's mistake; [81] otherwise Augustus would not have condemned the ten-year-old *Ars*. He approves of Wheeler's translation: ". . . when she was indicted with me for a joint crime." [82] Schanz, too, asserts that these words mean that the *Ars* and the mistake are joined and do not stand separately.[83]

On the other hand, when Ovid claims that the *Ars* is his accomplice in crime, Cocchia believes that he means the crime was simply the *Ars* itself—and nothing more—[84] though Owen's version of this passage has it that the charge of adultery against the *Ars* reflected upon the author of that book as a past offense which constituted, as it were, a kind of criminal record making his guilt seem more probable when he was accused of recent misconduct. According to Owen, therefore, no reference is implied in these lines to that recent fault of Ovid's.[85] These contradictory interpretations of the same verses demonstrate that Ovid has, to this day, eluded expert attempts to give them an unequivocal meaning.

III
Errant Poems

THE ARS AMATORIA

About A.D. I or 2 [86] the *Ars amatoria* made its debut into that glittering Roman society whose refinements of luxury contrasted violently with early Republican simplicity. The daring theme of this witty poem and its solemn parody of the didactic tradition assured it instant popularity, but the ever-watchful conservative element frowned (*Rem Am.* 361–398) upon this mockery of ancient Roman virtues. For this reason some scholars argue that the *Ars* was so great an affront to the spirit of Augustus' moral reforms that it was the sole reason for Ovid's downfall.[87] Others claim more moderately that this same reason makes it certainly the most important cause for Ovid's ruin.[88]

Augustus did what he could to restore the Roman integrity that had well-nigh vanished along with the Republic. Wealth and power, and the decimations of foreign and civil wars, had effectively corrupted and diminished both the Roman aristocracy and the common Roman stock. No means that might bring the Romans back to the straight-and-narrow path of their admired ancestors was neglected by Augustus. He threatened and cajoled, passed laws and encouraged the writing of great patriotic literature—all to little avail. Having tasted the riches that the rest of the world had to offer, the Roman people were understandably loth to return to the frugal habits and simple outlook of their forefathers. The consequence was that the laws of Augustus designed to encourage marriage and the bearing of children or to discourage adultery and luxury, were honored mainly in the breach, and by none more by Augustus and his family. For Augustus' pretense of restoring the Republic was paralleled by his pretense of restoring Republican morals. His example was as effective in hindering the latter restoration as his machinations were to prevent the former. As an empire-builder his magnificent achievement is unquestioned. He seems to have inspired selfless loyalty in the talented men who served him, although he certainly roused implacable hatred in his foes, among whom were sincere men of the highest caliber.

Yet, insofar as he figures in Ovid's life, Augustus necessarily shows another facet of his character, less admirable perhaps, but a typical sample of the weakness human nature is heir to whatever be the glory of its gifts. An incident illumines this flaw: Divorce was an ordinary and accepted practice among Roman nobility if, for instance, a new marriage might cement an important political alliance, or recoup a family fortune. Augustus treated his own daughter, Julia, as a political pawn by marrying her off several times solely to ensure the succession of his family to power, which may help to explain her unconventional behavior. He had shocked Rome when he divorced his wife, Scribonia, and forced Tiberius Claudius Nero to give up to him his six-months-pregnant wife, Livia. Augustus married Livia and three months later sent the new baby back to its father. Though Livia remained faithful to Augustus through fifty years, she had the undeniably strong motivation of her ambition to sustain her. For Augustus could be shameless in his pursuit of other women. Maecenas, his friend and competent adviser, had to stand by while the Emperor openly corrupted his wife, Terentia, and made her his mistress.

Augustus has been charged—sometimes unfairly—with greater crimes, as we shall see, but the instances adduced

are well-attested and seem characteristic. Yet he was not
satisfied with the morals and mores of the rest of the Roman
nobility. He enacted extensive legislation to improve the
status of marriage and of children and to eradicate adultery.
Doubtless, he was as sincere in this as he could be. But
the Romans had merely to look at his own behavior and
that of his family if they needed encouragement to circum-
vent the laws. Though Livia had no children by Augustus,
she was awarded, by legal fiction, the hard-earned privileges of those who actually had the legal minimum of three
children. Augustus' niece, the younger Antonia, retired to
the country when her husband died and did not marry again,
contrary to her uncle's law that required widows to marry
after two years. Both Julias, daughter and granddaughter
of Augustus, were guilty of adultery more than once, but
they had much company among the noble ladies of their set.
Strangely, the Julias both suffered severely at Augustus' unrelenting hands, though he spared other noble women guilty
of the same offense. But it is not unusual to condemn most
harshly in others—especially if they are close kin—what one
is guilty of oneself.

Considering this, it is scarcely credible that the *Ars* could
have shocked Augustus, particularly since he quite probably
tried his hand at turning out verses in the same vein.[89] Besides, if he felt that Ovid's poem was harmful to his official
programs for the reform of marriage and other social institutions, it is strange, to say the least, that a man of his unde-
niable administrative genius and adroitness should have tol-
erated its deleterious influence for nearly ten years.[90] When
he did reach the book-burning point, why does it appear that
he merely banished the *Ars* from the few public libraries
then in existence? [91] In short, Augustus punished Ovid far
too severely and much too late, if the *Ars amatoria* was the
real cause of this punishment.[92] By the same token, Ovid's
poetry cannot be considered even as the most important

cause of his relegation. Moreover, such an hypothesis would
have to explain away the clear statement in #20.

Perhaps there is no way of determining precisely how
much the *Ars* had irritated Augustus, since he may have been
nursing a concealed resentment against the author of this
poem, and Ovid's mistake may have triggered a long-re-
strained eruption of the emperor's feelings.[93] Nevertheless,
Ovid's constant references to his poetry, especially to the
Ars, leave little doubt that this poem was an official cause,
if not the only official cause, of his punishment.[94] Ovid
would not so often defend his writing on the one hand and
accuse it on the other, were this not so.[95] But Ovid's insistence on this point must be considered in the light of his
clear statement that his *error* was one which he dared not
describe, let alone defend. He could not accuse Augustus of
hypocrisy, and it may be that by defending his poetry he
was disingenuously focusing the attention of his reader on
the secret crime, thus bringing an indirect pressure on Augustus, who presumably was unwilling to explain or admit the
nature of the secret.

THE METAMORPHOSES

Though Ovid blames the *Ars amatoria* alone among his
poems for his relegation, some modern scholars have not
hesitated to indict other works as being equally to blame
and thus, perhaps, partly responsible for the relegation.
Rand, for instance, singles out the *Metamorphoses* because
it is irreligious.[96] Marót also points to this same work, but
because it is a mockery of high society.[97] Although the *Metamorphoses* was not formally published at the time of Ovid's
relegation, a few private copies were doubtless in circulation
among his friends (T. I, 7. 15 ff.). It is, therefore, not impossible that Augustus had seen the work. But this is scant

and dubious ground for singling out the *Metamorphoses* as
the object of his anger. One might also argue that Ovid
made the gesture of burning his copy of this particular work
precisely to propitiate Augustus and, perhaps, win his pardon. But, if Ovid were so intent upon winning pardon, surely
he would have changed and amended the offending themes
and passages and published the poem in a form more ac-
ceptable to Augustus. Furthermore, he would have cast
blame upon this work as he does upon his *Ars amatoria*.
But he does not once mention the *Metamorphoses* in this
connection. Because this latter work could have been defended far more easily, both on the grounds that the contents were myth for which Ovid could not be held responsible
and on the plea that he had attempted to withdraw the book,
his silence on this point must be conclusive.

IV

Cherchez la Femme

The official pretext for the exile of Ovid seems to have been that he had written the *Ars amatoria,* a poem subversive to morals because it taught the arts of adultery. Despite Ovid's protestations, which, when strictly interpreted, assert only that his own conduct had caused no scandal and that no Roman husband had occasion to wonder whether his wife's child was begotten by Ovid (T. II, 350–352), the reader of the poem naturally assumes that its author must have been experienced in all forms of seduction. Indeed, in admittedly autobiographical verse Ovid expresses himself in terms that, taken in their simple and obvious meaning, could be construed as a confession that he was guilty of adultery with at least one married woman.[98] These facts would automatically suggest to an otherwise uninformed scholiast, particularly in the Middle Ages when adultery was a favorite explanation of almost any unusual conduct or historical puzzle,[99] that the secret offense to which Ovid refers was also adultery. From this premise it would be a natural inference, given the severity of Ovid's punishment, that the lady whom he seduced was in some way closely related to the emperor who inflicted the punishment.

When Ovid was exiled, there was in the ruling family a handful of women with any one of whom the poet could have become involved. A prime suspect, of course, is Julia, Augustus' only child, born to him in 39 B.C., on the day that he divorced her mother, Scribonia, for immoral behavior. When Julia was fourteen, she was married to Marcellus, the

seventeen-year-old son of Augustus' sister, Octavia. This was
in 25 B.C., and M. Agrippa, the emperor's right-hand man,
presided at the ceremony. Though the marriage marked the
young man as Augustus' chosen successor, the fates decreed
otherwise when he died two years later. In 21 B.C., Augustus
chose the forty-two-year-old M. Agrippa as Julia's next husband. She was eighteen at this time and proceeded to bear
three sons and two daughters to Agrippa. Plutarch (*Ant.* 87)
maintains that Octavia suggested this marriage to keep
Livia's son, Tiberius, from marrying Julia, even though it
meant that Agrippa would have to divorce her own daughter, Marcella. Dio (LIV, 6. 6) merely says that Maecenas
advised the marriage because Agrippa had become so important. Agrippa died in 12 B.C. and Tiberius won the matri-
monial sweepstakes when Augustus ordered him to divorce
his beloved wife, Vipsania (a daughter of Agrippa), to marry
Julia. To Tiberius, Julia bore one son who died in infancy.
Whether she grew tired of being a shuttlecock in the game
of imperial succession or whether she was following the
bloodlines of her mother and father, Julia became notorious
for her love affairs in the years that followed. Tiberius would
no longer live with her and in 2 B.C. her escapades enraged
her father, though some say that Livia triggered the ex-
plosion hoping thereby to prejudice the chance for succession of Julia's two sons by Agrippa. Augustus sent his daughter into exile, where she died in A.D. 14, only a few months
after her father.

By Agrippa, Julia had a namesake daughter who was married when she was almost fifteen years old to L. Aemilius
Paulus, who became consul in A.D. 1. About A.D. 8—the date
is intriguing—Augustus learned that she was no better than
her mother and, in a fit of rage, confiscated her property,
forbade recognition of her children, tore her house down
and condemned her to exile, where she died twenty years
later.

Antonia, the younger of two daughters by that name, was born in 36 B.C. to Octavia and M. Antony. In 16 B.C. she was married to Nero Claudius Drusus, son of Livia by her marriage to Tiberius Claudius Nero, and had three children —Germanicus, Livilla, and Claudius, later emperor. When her husband died in 9 B.C., Antonia retired to the country, never to marry again. She grew old gracefully, honored and admired, and died in A.D. 37.

Livilla, her daughter (also called Livia), was born about 13 B.C. and was first married to Gaius Caesar, son of Julia and Agrippa. After Gaius died in A.D. 4, she married Tiberius' son, Drusus. Drusus died in A.D. 23 and Livilla was executed in A.D. 31 for having poisoned him at the behest of Sejanus, Tiberius' fellow-consul, who seduced her in the hope of marrying her and thus obtaining the succession after Tiberius. Unfortunately for his plans, Tiberius would not give him permission to marry Livilla precisely because her pedigree was too good for him. Later her mother, Antonia, warned Tiberius that Sejanus was plotting against him.

About 14 B.C. Julia and Agrippa had another daughter, Agrippina, who married Germanicus, a son of Antonia and Drusus. Six of their nine children survived. Agrippina was a proud, ambitious woman and when the popular Germanicus died in A.D. 19, she was sure that Tiberius had had him murdered. Since Sejanus regarded her and her sons as a menace to his plot to succeed Tiberius, he easily maneuvered Tiberius into banishing (in A.D. 29) this woman who so openly opposed him as her husband's murderer. She starved to death in A.D. 33 on the same island, Pandateria, to which Augustus had banished Julia, his daughter and her mother.

Of Antonia, the older daughter of Octavia and M. Antony we have small knowledge. She was born in August or September of 39 B.C. She married L. Domitius Ahenobarbus and gave him three children. Her son, Cn. Domitius, was the father of the notorious emperor, Nero.

Little information is available about Octavia's two daughters by her first husband, Caius Claudius Marcellus. Both were named Marcella and about one of them we know only that she existed. The other was the wife, in turn, of Agrippa and of Iullus Antonius, son of M. Antony, to whom her mother had once been married. Marcella bore Iullus a son, Lucius, and lost her husband in 2 B.C. when he committed suicide after being convicted of adultery with Julia, Augustus' daughter.

Last comes Livia who married Tiberius Claudius Nero when she was sixteen and gave him two sons, Tiberius, the future emperor, and Nero Claudius Drusus, father of the Emperor Claudius. In 38 B.C., when she was thirty-seven years old, Augustus took her away from her husband and married her himself. She died in A.D. 29, after a half century of successful political machinations on behalf of Augustus and her son, Tiberius.

These are the women—all of them related in some degree to Augustus—with whom Ovid may have become involved. Some of them figure largely in the hypotheses, others not at all. In no case can we deny the possibility of involvement. Yet it remains, for lack of evidence, a possibility only. Indeed, for some of the ladies in question, it is less than that. At any rate, Ovid's words, together with the gravity of his punishment, may have been the origin of all of the hints and statements that Ovid's offense was an adulterous relationship with a woman close to Augustus. Granted our purpose in the present study, and in view of the possibility that late scholia may contain some vestiges of authentic tradition, we must examine each of the identifications of the woman in question.

In our examination we shall have to distinguish clearly, although scholiasts and some modern scholars do not, between two distinct kinds of statement, that is, between a statement that Ovid did commit adultery with a given woman and a statement that adultery was his secret *error* or at least a cause of his exile.

CORINNA

Our second oldest testimonium—#2—concerning the exile of Ovid, and possibly the source of all the later traditions concerning adultery as the cause of Ovid's exile, consists of four lines by which Sidonius Apollinaris, Bishop of Clermont, alludes to Ovid in the course of a kind of catalogue of great writers. Since the exact implications of the Latin will be important, we shall, for convenience, quote the verses again:

> Et te carmina per libidinosa
> Notum, Naso tener, Tomosque missum,
> Quondam Caesareae nimis puellae
> Ficto nomine subditum Corinnae.

This passage raises three distinct questions: (1) How well informed was Sidonius? (2) Are the last two lines an explanation of the word that precedes them, *missum,* or do they merely record a third detail of Ovid's life logically unrelated to the two that preceded it? (3) What does *Caesarea puella* mean?

(1) Sidonius lived almost four hundred and fifty years after the death of Ovid. Although a man of unusual culture and learning in his time, Sidonius lived in an age of extreme decadence, at the very end of the Roman Empire in the West, when the body of literature, like all the other elements of civilization, was rapidly contracting. A pseudo-intellectual pretentiousness served more and more to conceal a mere modicum of knowledge, ill-digested and distorted by credulity and negligence. The Bishop did not escape the intellec-

tual vices of his time, and his reputation for scholarship is not of the best.[100] Understandably, therefore, his statement is regarded with suspicion.[101] Even if we grant that he reported accurately what he found in some source available to him but lost to us, that source may have been one of the rhetorical lives used in the schools of that day,[102] that were more notable for glib and fanciful explanations than for historical accuracy.

We are not encouraged by Sidonius' only other reference to Ovid, which informs us that "saepe versum Corinna cum suo Nasone complevit." [103] This statement, in itself astonishing,[104] is even more so in its context, for it introduces a kind of catalogue of literary ladies, including even Polla Argentaria,[105] who performed the same service for their lovers. Although we are prepared to believe that some of the women named were poetesses, the catalogue overstrains our credulity, if we take Sidonius' words literally. Hence, we are forced to conclude that he either let his imagination run away with him or that he produced one of the contorted metaphors that so frequently make his meaning obscure or unintelligible. If by *versum complevit* he intended to say nothing more than that the ladies of his catalogue were a source of literary inspiration to their lovers, he merely stated the obvious.[106]

Nevertheless, no matter how solid our grounds for regarding Sidonius as an unreliable witness, we cannot exclude the possibility that he, like other witnesses whose veracity or judgment we have reason to suspect, may be reporting accurately a detail which we have no means of verifying or disproving. The mere fact that his statement breaks what is for us the silence of almost five centuries [107] is not adequate grounds for incredulity, for we cannot know what was in the many works to which he had access that are lost to us. For example, we cannot prove that his source was not Suetonius' biography of Ovid. We dare not accept as true an unsup-

ported statement by Sidonius, but it would be rash to ignore
it as false. He may have been guessing,[108] or he may have
been reporting what was in his day accepted, with or without substantial reason and good authority, as an obvious
datum of literary history.

(2) In the last analysis, therefore, all that Sidonius really
tells us is that Ovid's mistress, celebrated in the *Amores,*
was a *Caesarea puella,* and that this fact, like Ovid's *carmina
libidinosa,* was somehow connected in Sidonius' mind with
Ovid's exile. We have, however, no means of knowing what
that connection was. It is possible, of course, that Sidonius
thought that Ovid's affair with Corinna was a cause of his
exile, but it is at least equally possible that he intended to
contrast the wretchedness of the poet in exile with the pros-
perous felicity that was his *quondam,* when he successfully
aspired to, and won as his mistress, a woman of the most
exalted family in the whole Roman Empire.

(3) Although Sidonius appears to have assumed that his
readers would at once understand his allusion, the words
Caesarea puella are for us disconcertingly imprecise. The
word *puella* must be understood freely; nothing can be made
of the argument that it strictly denotes an unmarried
woman,[109] whether slave or free, for it is used in Latin erotic
poetry with approximately the meaning of "girl" in the col-
loquial sense in which that word is currently used on a col-
lege campus or street corner. It is the word that Roman
amatory poets normally use with reference to their mistresses,
whatever the social or marital status of the woman in question.[110] Sidonius, therefore, merely tells us that Ovid had a
mistress who was *Caesarea.*

The adjective, *Caesarea,* however, is not free from am-
biguity. The English reader, mindful of the use of such ad-
jectives as "regal" or "queenly" in Romantic poetry to describe a woman's charms of person and manner, without
reference to her ancestry, and aware of Sidonius' propensity

to adorn the obvious with metaphorical obscurity, will wonder—although the question does not seem previously to
have been raised—whether Sidonius may not be attempting
a metaphor here. For this, it must be noted, there is no precedent in Latin usage. We may assume that the elaborate com-
pilations made for the *Thesaurus Linguae Latinae* provided
a comprehensive survey of the way in which this word is
used and the meanings which it carries.[111] Careful study of
these examples justifies the conclusion that there is no basis
for a metaphorical use of the adjective in the sense of English "queenly" or as a term of general praise. We must therefore conclude that Sidonius meant to say that Corinna was
in some way connected with the family of Augustus.

It has been argued that we should understand the phrase
to mean that Corinna was merely a freedwoman or slave in
the household of Augustus.[112] But this interpretation, which
may have seemed necessary to our forefathers on the grounds
that any other would imply a socially shocking *mésalliance,*
seems forced in an age which has witnessed not only scandal-
ous conduct on the part of a royal princess, but even a marriage between a woman who was once the heiress apparent
to what may have been the greatest throne then left in the
world and a notorious *débauché* of hybrid and plebian origin who has not even literary talent to recommend him. Although *puer* is sometimes a synonym of *servus,*[113] *puella* is
not a synonym of *ancilla,* and even if it were, we must here
understand the word in the sense that it has in erotic poetry.
While *Caesareus* can, of course, indicate ownership or pro-
prietorship with a suitable noun (for example, *Caesareus
veredus, Caesarea domus*), the normal and almost necessary meaning here is that Corinna was *Caesarea* because she
was related to Caesar by blood, adoption, marriage, or
amatory connection. And, so, even apart from the consideration that Sidonius would not have thought remarkable an
affair with a mere servant, which certainly would not have

been a cause of exile and as certainly could not have been regarded as a particular distinction or felicity, we must conclude that Sidonius meant that Corinna stood in some close personal relation to Augustus.

We may note in passing that the rest of Sidonius' statement is not entirely free from difficulty, although not such as would affect the question in which we are interested. *Subditum,* for instance, though it means strictly "bound to," "submissive to," "obedient to," is often translated in this context as "enamored of." Whatever objection might be made to this latter translation,[114] the word is indeed applicable to the relationship in which the Latin amatory poets stood, or professed to stand, to their *dominae.* Even *nimis* can be a puzzle, since it may have its normal meaning of "excessively" or the weakened meaning in late Latin of "very much." If the former is Sidonius' intention, why then, does he think Ovid's emotion excessive? Nonetheless, no matter how we skirmish with the words, we cannot obscure the contiguity of the verses and the association of ideas they naturally suggest.[115]

POETIC FANTASY

The notion that any certainty can be reached about Corinna's existence—and, *a fortiori,* her identity—has been dismissed as hopeless,[116] a conclusion with which Ovid himself might concur. Twenty years from the time he first began writing about Corinna, he reports that people are still wondering who she was (*A.A.* III, 538): [117]

> Et multi, quae sit nostra Corinna, rogant.

Martial was so piqued by this mystery and Ovid's boasts of world-wide fame that he wrote in irritation a paradoxical reversal of the boast (*Epig.* V, 10. 10): [118]

Norat Nasonem sola Corinna suum.

Such was Corinna's plasticity that one noble lady—obviously craving any sort of attention, not excepting notoriety—felt no qualms about posing as Corinna (*Am.* II, 17, 29), because she was well aware that no one could detect her imposture through Ovid's verses. For what Ovid says of Corinna might well be said of any girl, since so much of his description may be classified as standard poetic exaggeration upon the theme of love.[119]

Though many students of this question have denied that Corinna was a fantasy of Ovid's mind,[120] scholars nowadays lean toward the idea that she is a creature of the poet's imagination,[121] no more than a theme, a central core, around which Ovid weaves diverse experiences and emotions. She herself has no reality apart from his pages.[122] Ovid would seem to lend credence to this opinion (T. II, 355):[123]

Magnaque pars mendax operum est et ficta meorum.

Recent research into the editions of the *Amores*, however, gives evidence that what has survived is a later edition revised by Ovid when he was about forty-five and which celebrates a variety of fair ladies, although the poet may have restricted the lost first edition to the praise of Corinna's charms alone, or at least given a more coherent picture of her.[124] If such be the case, then the traditional arguments against the reality of Corinna lose much of their force and cogency.

BIOGRAPHICAL EVIDENCE

Though a comparison between the facts of Julia's life and Ovid's description of Corinna should prove enlightening, we must keep in mind that Corinna is mentioned by name in only eleven of the forty-nine poems which comprise the *Amores.*[125] This, coupled with the probability that at least several fair ladies are immortalized in our present edition, should urge us to great caution in attributing to Corinna everything that Ovid sings concerning his lady loves. Consequently, the comparison which follows is merely tentative and subject to the correction which further research into this particular aspect of *Quaestiones Ovidianae* may make necessary.

Corinna—if, indeed, it is she—was married to quite an old man, if the poet is to be believed; his words, though, may reflect merely the spitefulness of youth, to whom all who are not very young are hopelessly ancient.[126] The truth is that Agrippa was only forty-two when Julia was wedded to him in 21 B.C.[127] Corinna had no children, lest her beauty suffer impairment (*Am.* II, 14. 7). On the contrary, Julia found her five children by Agrippa, three boys and two girls (Suet. *Aug.* 64), no impediment to her attractiveness. Corinna had a sister (*Am.* I, 8. 91), Julia had none (Suet. *Aug.* 63). Corinna was served by a eunuch and maids, but this was common among upper class Romans.[128] Corinna was almost bald from frequent dyeing of her hair (*Am.* I, 14. 1), while Julia's hair began to turn prematurely white (Mac. *Sat.* II, 5. 7). If some resemblance between the heads of hair is here uncovered, that is purely accidental and, considering Ovid's poetical license, it may even be imaginary.[129] Reverting to Corinna's husband once more, Ovid makes of him a figure of fun and insult (*Am.* I, 4: III, 4), a risky act considering the possibility that the highly placed Agrippa might somehow learn the secret, if he were the lady's spouse. Ovid and Corinna go to the same games together (*Am.* III, 2. 20). Corinna comes to him, not he to her (*Am.* I, 5. 9) —this circumstance could imply that her social station was such that he could not openly visit her alone. Ovid tears her hair in anger (*Am.* I, 7. 49); he laments her selling of her charms like a common prostitute (*Am.* III, 12. 10); he chides her for boasting widely of her prowess in the bed (*Am.* III, 14, 15–16, 27–28), but this would not be inconsistent with the character of Julia.

If Corinna and Julia are identical, some of these verses are nettles to handle, and Huber is of the opinion that a great deal of unsatisfactory explanation is needed to account for a royal princess behaving in this manner with an unknown man of rather low social station; [130] but even greater social disparity has been, and is, common.

Whenever the poets of Rome were bent upon enshrining the charms of their true loves in perennial verse, they customarily and considerately substituted pseudonyms which were the metrical equivalent of the ladies' real names. [131] Since, in the present case, the names of Julia (-uu) and Corinna (u-u) do not match metrically, this discrepancy has been used to deny their identity categorically. [132] Rules, however, do admit of exceptions, so there is a possibility that the metrical dissimilarity might be explained away in this instance. Nonetheless, the metrical evidence, so far as it goes, tends against the identification.

AUGUSTUS' REACTION

Credulity is further strained by the effort to believe that Augustus could have remained in ignorance for some twenty years that his daughter Julia and Ovid's Corinna were one and the same woman. [133] And if the secret was not discovered at the time Julia was exiled in 2 B.C., it is highly improbable that it would have come to light—or been much regarded even by Augustus—ten years later.

CONTRADICTIONS

Assuming, for the sake of discussion, that Corinna and Julia were one person, and that Augustus learned of this fact, the difficulties in this theory are not thereby swept aside. Would Ovid, with the intention of obtaining pardon, so constantly remind Augustus that he had been instrumental in the moral breakdown of his daughter? This is improbable in the highest degree.[134] And why did the emperor wait ten years to punish Ovid when Julia and all of her other paramours were sentenced at once? Only Ovid was left untouched. Only his name is not mentioned by Velleius Paterculus (I, 2. 50) in the catalogue of Julia's lovers. If Ovid were in truth guilty, then his punishment was not severe enough. If he was guilty solely of causing suspicion that Corinna and Julia were the same person,[135] then he was punished too severely, for Augustus confirmed all possible suspicions about his daughter's delinquency (Sen. *De Ben.* VI, 32): [136] "Flagitia principalis domus in publicum emisit."

Ovid refrains from regret of any sort over Corinna. If she was real—and truly Julia—then Ovid's lack of remorse might be due to the fact that the affair was long over and he could excuse his fault on the grounds that he was a youth at the time of the error. Otherwise, Ovid was not the sort of person to stay his pen from lamentations over the cause of ruin to his life. On the contrary, he appears to be rather proud of the *Amores* (T. IV, 10. 57–62): [137]

> Carmina cum primum populo iuvenalia legi,
>   Barba resecta mihi bisve semelve fuit.
> Moverat ingenium totam cantata per urbem
>   Nomine non vero dicta Corinna mihi.
> Multa quidem scripsi, sed, quae vitiosa putavi,
>   Emendaturis ignibus ipse dedi.

If the *Amores* had been the cause of his downfall, as one scholiast (#10) confidently declares, Ovid would scarcely refer to them with such evident satisfaction.

Ovid crowns all with the cogent point that he made his mistake in his old age (#37). But Corinna, be she fact or fancy, is definitely an episode of his youth. Therefore, if Ovid's adultery is recent, then Corinna, whoever she was, is entirely excluded.

This, though, opens the door to the younger Julia and Livilla and others. Of course, the younger Julia cannot possibly be Corinna, to whom Ovid first began penning lines about 25 B.C., some six years before this granddaughter of Augustus was born (Dio LIV).[138] Someone has ventured a surmise that Livia may have been the true Corinna, but the potent arguments against a royal princess filling the role of Corinna militate a hundred times more against the idea of the empress herself being Ovid's concubine, especially since Tacitus (*Ann.* V, 1) praises rather than impugns the integrity of her private life.

In an age lacking the advantages of modern techniques and materials for literary criticism, the idea that Corinna was one of the Julias, or even Livia, aroused no great scepticism,[139] but today's accumulation of several more centuries' worth of data to draw upon, plus more developed methods for handling it, have done much to discredit this theory. Little remains of the affirmative position except that Julia, the emperor's daughter, and Ovid were, indeed, about the same age.[140] It seems improbable that any relation will ever be discovered between Corinna and Ovid's secret error.

LIVIA

Not a few of the testimonia—namely, ##5, 7, 8, 11, 13, and possibly #6 and #9—[141] concerning Ovid's secret *error* attribute his fall to a too intimate association with the empress Livia. For several reasons this suggestion fails to convince. The ages of the persons concerned—Ovid was fifty and Livia about sixty-seven in A.D. 8—constitute a hurdle difficult even for a credulous mind to leap. Above all stands Livia's reputation for unblemished fidelity to Augustus.[142] Such statements about Livia and Ovid by these medieval scholiasts may well stem from simple inattention to chronology. The quality of their imagination, as well as the freedom with which they exercised it, appears clearly in #5, which is obviously a mere transposition into Roman history of the story of Joseph and Potiphar's wife.

There is a bare possibility, however, that a germ of ancient gossip could have survived in the scholia which accuse Ovid of a liaison with Livia, for the latter was the name not only of Augustus' wife, but of her granddaughter, who was also Augustus' grandniece. The name of this young lady, who would have been about twenty-one years old in A.D. 8,[143] appears to have been "Livia," although she is frequently referred to as Livilla. She was the daughter of Nero Claudius Drusus and Antonia Minor, and was married first to Gaius Caesar and then to Drusus, the son of Tiberius. Her morals appear not to have been of the best, for she was executed in A.D. 31 for helping to poison her husband at the instigation of Sejanus, who had seduced her.[144] Obviously, Livilla could not be Corinna, because, like the younger Julia, she was not born at the time that the *Amores* were written, but it is not impossible that she could have had an affair with Ovid at the time of his relegation, or that at least Roman gossip could have supposed so. We cannot, therefore, entirely exclude the possibility that the scholiasts' imaginations were stimulated by some morsel of ancient information, but it remains a mere possibility, unsupported by even a gleam of other evidence. And we dare not trust a race of reckless charlatans.[145]

JULIA,
THE GRANDDAUGHTER OF AUGUSTUS

Since the association of Ovid with the younger of the two Julias will receive detailed consideration in the next chapter, we need here point out only that she is said to have been Ovid's mistress, which is possible, and also (#10) Corinna, which is fantastic. The later popularity of the hypothesis that Ovid was her lover arises from a coincidence of dates, for Julia and Ovid were both exiled from Rome within the same year. This hypothesis has been reinforced by the fact that Julia was notorious for her adulteries—why not a poet, too? —and was publicly disgraced and exiled when her conduct at last forced itself upon the attention of her grandfather. Beyond this, there is no evidence to support the conjecture.

OTHER "CAESAREAE PUELLAE"

Huber suggests that Ovid may have dallied with one of the ladies attached to the staff which served and cared for the ruling family.[146] This, obviously, is possible but could not be a cause of relegation, for in that case Ovid would have endured a punishment out of all proportion to the crime—if crime it could be called—of carrying on an affair with one of the help.

The possibility remains, of course, that Ovid may have gotten himself mixed up with one of Augustus' mistresses, a not wholly improbable notion on the basis of the information provided by Suetonius and Tacitus as to the emperor's lifelong devotion to amatory diversions.

CONCLUSION

Sidonius' story about Corinna's being a *Caesarea puella* cannot be disproved, in which case she had nothing to do with
Ovid's exile, except on the supposition that she was Augustus' daughter and so accounted for his rancor against Ovid
at the time of the exile. Under these circumstances, there is
naturally no allusion by Ovid to the affair, unless we want to
read some significance into his protest that no one knew who
Corinna was.

Taking the other thesis that Ovid was, shortly before his
exile, guilty of adultery with Julia the Younger, or with
Livilla, we may submit that this is an entirely gratuitous
hypothesis, suggested only by statements, most of which are
impossible in the form in which they are made, and that are
likely to have been merely inferences drawn rashly and without regard for chronology, from the lines in Sidonius.

One insuperable obstacle looms, above all, before the
eyes of anyone who wishes to postulate, or intends to prove,
that Ovid committed adultery and was, accordingly, punished for that crime. Ovid is at great pains to make clear that
he in no way perpetrated a wrong, except, possibly, by the
use of his eyes. For this reason, we may be sure that the
secret *error,* which was presumably the major cause of Ovid's
exile, cannot have been adultery, since this sin is decidedly
not committed with the eyes. Also, except in the lurid story
of Hostius Quadra, told by Seneca (*Quaest. nat.* I, 16),
people do not watch themselves commit adultery.

V
May and December

A popularity poll of the hypotheses about the nature of Ovid's secret mistake would doubtless reveal that the majority relate it, one way or another, to Julia, the granddaughter of Augustus. Suspicion stems from the penalties imposed upon Julia and Ovid, who were punished at approximately the same time and upon somewhat similar grounds. The emperor charged Ovid with generally encouraging adultery by his *Ars amatoria,* as is clear from #47, while Julia was accused of adultery (Tac. *Ann.* IV, 71). Perhaps Ovid inadvertently witnessed an immoral act between the princess and one of her lovers, who is usually identified as the only one whose name is known to us, Decimus Junius Silanus, but sometimes as her own brother, Agrippa Postumus.[147] Ovid may have been so indiscreet as to aid and abet the affair. Or, if Julia were merely stimulated and encouraged in her improper behavior by reading the *Ars amatoria,* he would be at least indirectly responsible for her conduct.

HISTORICAL EVIDENCE

This hypothesis rests primarily upon the temporal relationship between Ovid's and Julia's punishments. Because Ovid was relegated in A.D. 8 and Julia seems to have been exiled to the island of Trimerus off Apulia in the same year (Tac. *Ann.* IV, 71), certain scholars have seized upon the apparent coincidence in timing to argue a causal, rather than a casual, connection between the two events. There are other arguments to support this idea, and these must be submitted, in due course, to examination. But first to be answered is the question: Were Julia and Ovid really punished almost simultaneously?

The brief mention of Julia's death in Tacitus is the only source from which to compute the year in which she was banished by her grandfather. The historian records (*Ann.* IV, 71. 4) that she died in the consulship of Junius Silanus and Silius Nerva toward the end of A.D. 28, twenty years after she was exiled; thus A.D. 8 would appear to be the year of the edict against Julia as well as against Ovid. It is well known, however, that historians from Herodotus to Toynbee have enjoyed certain traditional liberties, such as their penchant for using round numbers. Tacitus could have been speaking in such numbers, and the actual time may have been nearer nineteen years or, worse, twenty-one years.[148] If not convincing, this line of inquiry does indicate at least the possibility of uncertainty in timing the edict against Julia.[149]

The dates of exile of two other individuals are important to this hypothesis. When did D. Silanus leave Rome as a voluntary exile (Tac. *Ann.* III, 24), and when was Agrippa Postumus banished to Surrentum and to Planasia (Suet. *Aug.* 65; Dio LV, 32)? To answer the last part of the question first, both Velleius Paterculus (II, 112) and Dio Cassius (LV, 32) agree that Agrippa was exiled in A.D. 7. What we know about D. Silanus, the brother of Marcus, comes from Tacitus. Silanus was not exiled, but merely deprived of the emperor's friendship, a measure he perceptively interpreted as a request for him to depart forthwith from Rome. Accordingly, he left the city of his own volition (Tac. *Ann.* 24), and, since Tacitus brackets him with Julia, it is a reasonable inference that his departure was roughly simultaneous with Julia's punishment; that is, she may have departed

Rome in the year A.D. 8; but he may also have gone in A.D. 7 or 9, if the "twenty years" of Julia's exile is merely an approximation. In that case, Ovid's implication as accessory to Silanus' crime with Julia would be a matter for strong scepticism.[150]

When all the dates are tabulated, Agrippa is seen to have been banished definitely in A.D. 7. This date should absolve him of involvement with Ovid, who was sentenced nearly a year later, except on the hypothesis that an affair between Julia and Agrippa came to light a year or so after the latter had been banished—perhaps by interrogation of servants concerned in a more recent adultery of Julia's. As already shown above, Ovid was clearly relegated toward the end of A.D. 8. Julia seems to have been exiled also in A.D. 8, but she may have been so punished either in A.D. 7 or 9. Silanus left Rome of his own accord, perhaps in A.D. 8, but he may have gone in A.D. 9, after Ovid was relegated; or he may have begun his journey in A.D. 7, before the edict against the famous poet was promulgated. In short, the chronological evidence invoked to bolster so many arguments would seem to add little to their solidity, since it does not itself rest upon unshakeable foundations.

PERSONAL RELATIONSHIPS

Our consideration centers next upon the complex, but interesting, problem of relationships and attitudes between the persons involved, according to the theory that links Julia and Ovid. Ten years prior to the incident, a chagrined Augustus had discovered that his daughter, also named Julia, was firmly addicted to promiscuous sexual activities (Dio LV, 10). Aroused to frustrated anger, he compelled her chief lover, Iullus Antonius, son of the famous triumvir, to commit suicide (Tac. *Ann.* I, 10). He merely banished her other lovers. Julia he exiled to the island of Pandateria and later to Rhegium (Suet. *Aug.* 65; Tac. *Ann.* I, 53). About this same time, Ovid first published his *Ars amatoria.*[151]

In this intricate puzzle both Julias were exiled, and Augustus published their crimes in each instance or, at least, did nothing to keep them a secret (Sen. *De Ben.* VI, 32. 1–2). When he died, his will contained instructions which forbade their burial in the family vaults (Suet. *Aug.* 101. 3). Why was the emperor lenient with the principal culprit, D. Silanus, in one case, yet implacable toward the other, Iullus Antonius? Ordinarily, the ties which bind father to daughter are stronger than those which join grandfather and granddaughter, and this may be the reason why Antonius was not spared. In addition, the decade which intervened between the two affairs may have mellowed the old emperor and reconciled him to the weight and prevalence of human weakness and perversity. More probably, however, Augustus was exercising political prudence. Had he exiled Antonius, instead of executing him, the doorway to rebellion would have been opened. For Antonius was the son of a deadly political foe and had a name which yet might raise legions. His exile might have attracted the powerful friends of his father to attempt to rescue him. Augustus would have had to punish these men as rebels, and they, knowing this, would have realized that successful rebellion was their only hope of survival. On the other hand, D. Silanus was the son of a very close friend of Augustus. This family had great influence and D. Silanus later became the uncle of Caligula's future wife and brother-in-law to the daughter of the younger Julia (Tac. *Ann.* 3. 23; Suet. *Gai. Calig.* 12). To alienate a loyal supporter by unnecessary severity toward his son would have been an act of folly that a prudent politician would have instinctively avoided. There is also evidence that Augustus really needed competent administrators.

Odder still is the question of Augustus' strictness with Ovid, who is usually considered to have been a mere witness of the crime, as contrasted with his mercy toward Silanus, the perpetrator of the deed; though Augustus did, at the time of his death, appear to be softening toward Ovid. More perplexing still, is the question of why Tiberius allowed Augustus' laws to be relaxed (Tac. *Ann.* III, 25) while he remained adamant to Ovid's pleas for mitigation of his sentence. Silanus was permitted to return from exile, admittedly on sufferance and after Ovid was dead (Tac. *Ann.* III, 24). Toward Ovid, Tiberius was unrelenting to the end.

THE PUNISHMENT OF OVID

Many reasons have been elaborated to explain the difference—strange by this hypothesis—in the fate of Ovid and of Silanus. Some believe that the Claudian Tiberius unbent for Silanus because through him a Julian had been brought low, while he hated Ovid for protecting one of that detested house by not reporting the affair at once.[152] According to others, Augustus excused Julia and Silanus because of their youth but struck the harder at Ovid because he was older and should have known better.[153] A few think that Augustus had a long-standing and secret resentment against Ovid occasioned by the publication of the immoral *Ars amatoria* ten years earlier.[154] Several theorists merely restate the hypothesis by claiming that Ovid may have suffered so severely because he was found to be implicated in the downfall of either Julia.[155] Certainly, Ovid would not even have made their aquaintance, were it not for his poetry,[156] so the two reasons for his downfall, his mistake and his *Ars amatoria* could be said to be united.[157] Another suggestion is that Ovid appeared to Augustus as the very incarnation of the corruption of the times.[158] Finally, the poet may have been treated so severely in order to silence him and to remove him as a reminder of a disgrace to the ruling family.[159]

Had Augustus truly intended to silence Ovid, the power of the centurion's sword or the assassin's dagger would have been invoked without hesitation.[160] Moreover, Ovid's part in the affair was already well known (#22), not, perhaps, to everyone, but certainly as current gossip in fashionable society. If silence and forgetfulness were the emperor's intent, Ovid himself frustrated the motive behind his relegation by a flood of letters filled with tantalizing allusions to his mistake and with appeals for mercy. But the crowning refutation of this argument is Augustus' own failure to take precautions which would conceal from the world the affairs in which each Julia was caught.[161] One does not silence a witness to what one publicly admits and laments.[162]

The description of Ovid as the image of corruption could apply only to his literary works, not to himself. His own life, he contends, was exemplary: (T. II, 349–360): [163]

> Sic ego delicias et mollia carmina feci,
>   Strinxerit ut nomen fabula nulla meum.
> Nec quisquam est adeo media de plebe maritus,
>   Ut dubius vitio sit pater ille meo.
> Crede mihi, distant mores a carmine nostro—
>   Vita verecunda est, Musa iocosa mea—
> Magnaque pars mendax operum est et ficta meorum:
>   Plus sibi permisit compositore suo.
> Nec liber indicium est animi, sed honesta voluntas
>   Plurima mulcendis auribus apta ferens.
> Accius esset atrox, conviva Terentius esset.
>   Essent pugnaces, qui fera bella canunt.

Augustus, too, in virtue of his office as Censor, had approved of Ovid's way of life (T. II, 89–103). Whatever reservations we may have about taking Ovid's protestations literally, it is scarcely possible that, in the Roman society of that age, he could have been so noted as a *débauché* as to make him seem on that ground more objectionable to Augustus than the adulterer himself.

The question is being begged with a vengeance, when the emperor's severity and vindictiveness toward Ovid is said to be explained by the circumstance that Ovid was implicated with his daughter and/or granddaughter.[164] This is precisely what the hypothesis endeavors to establish.

Granted that Ovid was older than Silanus or the young Julia by about thirty years, and that he should have known better than to get mixed up in their affairs, his gray hairs alone could not have merited an incomparably severer punishment, especially if he was a mere witness. Ovid would have been the first to complain—or at least to hint—to Augustus that he was punished the most, though guilty the least.[165] Silanus, too, would have faced the brunt of his literary indignation, but Ovid does not even name him.[166] Though the historians, who display no hesitation about mentioning Silanus, name no accomplices, such restraint may mean that there were none to be named.[167] It means certainly that if there were others, the historians either did not know their identities or thought them persons too obscure to be mentioned. If the accomplice was Ovid, it is strange that Tacitus, an alert critic of imperial transgressions and inconsistencies, should have overlooked an opportunity to make a telling point.[168]

Whatever Ovid's mistake was, he could not have been a mere witness of the affairs of Julia the Younger, for witnesses are not in danger of death, when the malefactor—in this case, Silanus—goes virtually free. Yet Ovid did think that he was in danger of losing his life for he so often thanks Augustus for sparing him (T. I, I. 20): [169]

> Id quoque, quod vivam, munus habere dei.

For the same reason—Silanus' relative impunity—it is not likely that Ovid's error consisted in aiding the progress of an affair between the young Julia and her lover. Despite this improbability, not a few of the hypotheses offer detailed de-

scriptions of the nature of Ovid's involvement with this
Julia. Alexander believes that Ovid's house was a rendezvous
for the "night club" set, so that he and his wife, on return-
ing from their vacation at the Nassau of their day, crossed
their threshold to discover a party in full swing and were
shocked to come upon the younger Julia in an extremely
compromising situation.[170] Meiser anticipated Alexander
with what is essentially the same idea.[171] That Julia, the
emperor's granddaughter, somehow employed Ovid to help
her carry on an intrigue is Rose's thesis;[172] Cartault and
others hold that Ovid accidentally saw this Julia in mid-
orgy;[173] Appel's surmise is that Ovid joined wholeheartedly
in the young woman's obscenities;[174] and Federico solemnly
explains that Ovid unwillingly saw the younger Julia and
her brother, Agrippa, in the act of incest, to which they
were incited by the verses which he had read to them at
dinner.[175]

LITERARY EVIDENCE

Certain Ovidian texts that bear immediately upon the nature
of his secret *error* are, quite naturally, woven into the argument of all hypotheses, however diverse their conclusions,
since these verses do, unfortunately, lend themselves to a
variety of interpretations. Thus each hypothesis necessarily
begins by laying a foundation of texts which are also the
bases of rival hypotheses. Examples of such passages are
(T. II, 103–106): [176]

> Cur aliquid vidi? Cur noxia lumina feci?
> Cur imprudenti cognita culpa mihi?
> Inscius Actaeon vidit sine veste Dianam:
> Praeda fuit canibus non minus ille suis.

and (T. III, 6. 35): [177]

Stultiamque meum crimen debere vocari,

and (T. IV, 4. 37): [178]

> Hanc quoque, qua perii, culpam scelus esse negabis
>   Si tanti series sit tibi nota mali.
> Aut timor aut error nobis, prius obfuit error.
>   A! sine me fati non meminisse mei;

Without exception, the advocate of each hypothesis tries to prove that such verses uniquely fit his own scheme relating to Ovid's mysterious dereliction. But the multiple meanings that result for the same passage seem effectively to cancel its probative force for any one hypothesis over the others. Although these lines neither prove nor disprove an association between Ovid and Julia the Younger, they do limit Ovid's possible role to that of witness. For, although an accessory in an adulterous intrigue between persons more powerful than he could claim that *timor* led him to serve them, he could not, without absurdity, pretend that he was *imprudens* ($=$ *inscius*) when he learned that adultery had taken place. *Imprudens* does not normally mean "imprudent," "without judgment"; the normal meaning, given by the *Thesaurus Linguae Latinae* is "unaware of" or "inexperienced in." *Inopinans, improvidus, inscius* are the words used by the *Thesaurus* to explain the meaning of *imprudens*.

In the poems written from exile, some verses demand our attention because they allude to the members of the ruling family in terms which are particularly inept, if Ovid and Julia were, in truth, associates in crime. These lines are (T. IV, 2. 11): [179]

> Cumque bonis nuribus pro sospite Livia nato,

and (P. II, 8. 46): [180]

> Cumque bonis nuribus quod peperere nurus,

and (P. II, 2. 73): [181]

Adde nurus neptesque pias natosque nepotum.

The first two pose no problem, for Julia, the daughter, was long since divorced from Tiberius, and Julia, the grand-daughter, was never married to any of Augustus' sons or grandsons.

The difficulty lies in the third of these verses, for, if Ovid's downfall were linked with the moral misconduct of the younger Julia, how could he muster the effrontery to refer to the *neptes pias,* who are Agrippina the elder, Livilla and Julia? Suppose that Julia's crime juridically removed her from the ruling family; nevertheless, such removal would remain a legal fiction, and psychological laws of association would insure each reader's instant recollection of the *"impia"* Julia.[182] No Roman would overlook the preposterous incongruity if Ovid, of all persons, called Julia, notorious for her excesses and her defiance of her father's laws and wishes, *"pia."* A few authors, indeed, go to the extreme of denying that Ovid wrote this, on the grounds that he was too great a master of language and urbanity to fall into so flagrant a *faux pas.*[183] But this is to beg the question, for the lines cannot be suspected on other grounds and there is no known motive for interpolation. Since the words do belong to Ovid, the inference to be drawn is that they make it, in all probability, psychologically impossible that he and the young Julia were partners in any way for their mutual ruin.

Another line sometimes cited in this connection is (T. IV, 10. 101): [184]

Quid referam comitumque nefas famulosque nocentes?

Again, the meaning is not so unequivocal that scholarly ingenuity has not been able to shape it to suit several hypotheses. Theories political,[185] religious,[186] and moral [187] have depended on this verse for reinforcement. In the present case, the argument would have it that friends and slaves of Ovid revealed his part in the affair with this Julia.[188] But the line almost certainly refers to what happened *after* Ovid had received the edict of relegation,[189] since he has just mentioned it and proceeds to complain that his friends have deserted him and that his slaves have behaved badly.[190] This construction gains support from a number of other loci, such as (P. II, 7. 61–62): [191]

> Recta fides comitum poterat mala nostra levare:
> Ditata est spoliis perfida turba meis;

or (P. II, 3. 29–30): [192]

> Cumque alii nolint etiam me nosse videri,
> Vix duo proiecto tresve tulistis opem;

and (T. I, 9. 5–6, 17–20): [193]

> Donec eris sospes, multos numerabis amicos:
> Tempora si fuerint nubila, solus eris
>
> .   .   .   .
>
> Dum stetimus, turbae quantum satis esset, habebat
> Nota quidem, sed non ambitiosa domus.
> At simul impulsa est, omnes timuere ruinam,
> Cautaque communi terga dedere fugae.

Finally, cognizance must be taken of the frequency with which Ovid refers to his *error*. Would the poet have hoped to obtain pardon by constantly reminding Augustus of a disgrace to his family which he himself had helped to bring about? [194] But if Ovid had remained silent, would the emperor in time have relented? Even this possibility does not seem likely in view of the fact that Augustus was known to be especially obdurate in matters affecting the honor of his family (Suet. *Aug.* 65). He had early lost patience with popular petitions for the return of his daughter from exile and had forbidden any more of them (Suet. *Aug.* 65).

AGRIPPA AND JULIA

To conclude this section, one more theory must be treated briefly. Ovid is thought to have encouraged by his poetry the act of incest between Agrippa Postumus and his sister, the younger Julia; [195] or, if he did not promote the act, he was, at any rate, a witness to it.[196] The origin of this idea is perhaps a scholium on the Satires of Juvenal (Schol. in Juv. *Sat.* VI, 158): "Iulia cum quo commisit incestum et propterea ab Augusto relegatus est." [197] The author of this comment may well have misunderstood *Amores* II, 5. 13–28. Tacitus (*Ann.* I, 3), however, affirms that Agrippa was not punished for any crime in which he was detected. To compound the difficulty, Agrippa was banished one year before Ovid, so it is something a problem to get the three together on the island of Planasia, whither he had been removed. From beginning to end, this idea has the appearance of pure invention—invention by a scholiast who obviously did not understand the line he was attempting to explain and was too uninformed to realize that neither Julia nor her brother could have been Jews or have lived in Palestine.[198]

CONCLUSION

Once the evidence for this relationship between the young Julia and Ovid has been sifted and sorted, what value has it for the argument? The historical facts are untouched. Ovid and this Julia seem to have been exiled from Rome about the same time, one for the alleged crime of teaching adultery, the other for definitely practicing it. Ovid and Julia were punished most severely; Silanus, by comparison, received but a warning. The attitudes of Augustus, Ovid, Tiberius, Julia, and Silanus toward one another are clear enough in some instances, but enlightening in none. The *Ars amatoria,* a bone of contention in this argument, had been in circulation about ten years before Ovid suffered for it.

These are the facts, some of them inimical to the hypothesis, some neutral, with only the contemporaneity of the banishments favoring it. The burden of the historical evidence, therefore, weighs, on the whole, against the hypothesis.

Furthermore, it is extremely unlikely that Augustus would have punished anyone who was not a member of his household for merely failing to report one of his granddaughter's adulteries; thus, the hypothesis that Ovid witnessed such a scene can be saved only by a further conjecture—that Julia's paramour was not Silanus but someone whom Ovid had not at the time, but might later have, identified and whom Augustus was, for whatever reason, determined to spare and protect.

VI

The Indiscreet Emperor

AUGUSTUS' PART IN OVID'S MISTAKE

The possibility that Augustus was directly involved in Ovid's *error* was not neglected by Bayle who suggested that Ovid may have chanced upon a scene of some delicacy.[199] He postulated that reports of a vexatious family problem reached Augustus who thereupon chose a discreet place for questioning his daughter, or one of her friends, in order to learn more about the matter—perhaps going so far as to threaten or strike her. Or he may have been dealing with a slave—even torturing him—for the same purpose. Perhaps he was merely weeping alone over the affair. But whatever Augustus was doing, Ovid's accidental intrusion upon the scene exasperated the emperor to the limit and the poet suffered correspondingly.

Not only does the punishment seem too severe, but sufficient reason is lacking for the grim vindictiveness of Augustus.[200] But most important, what weakens this hypothesis is the fact that no crime was involved,[201] since what Augustus was doing was in no sense a crime; yet Ovid saw a crime committed.

Dio Cassius (LVI, 43) recounts an incident which some have espoused as a likely cause for Ovid's relegation: Athenodorus became so worried about Augustus' safety that he disguised himself as a woman and had himself transported inside a closed litter into Augustus' private apartments, where he leaped forth, sword in hand, to urge Augustus to be more careful about his security, having just proved how easy it was to attack him by means of this customary procedure of the palace. Ovid witnessed this scene and was packed off to Tomis. The first jarring note is struck when Dio relates that Augustus thanked Athenodorus for his concern and promised to take proper precautions in the future. This being so, the emperor could scarcely thank the leading character while punishing an innocent onlooker;[202] and how could Ovid claim that he deserved death?[203] Besides, this whole incident, as related by Dio, may be nothing more than an anecdote.[204]

Some authors have not shrunk from intimating that Ovid caught Augustus in the commission of some such practice as pederasty,[205] which might account for the emperor's wrath, for Aristotle says (*Rhet.* II, 4–5) that the greatest hatred is generated when a person is surprised *in delicto flagrante*. Suetonius' testimony (*Aug.* 67–71) indicates that Augustus may have been capable of such acts, and pseudo Aurelius Victor would seem to corroborate the opinion of Suetonius by claiming (*Epit de Caes.* I, 22, 24) that the emperor was harsh toward sexual immorality in others because he himself was so immoral in that regard. But if Augustus was involved, he cannot have known that Ovid witnessed his offense until some time later—presumably after Ovid had told others, if he spoke about it at all. The only reasonable course for Augustus in such a situation is either to assassinate the witness before he can speak or else to ignore him and hope that his report will be dismissed as idle gossip or malicious invention.

If Ovid wished to gain a pardon, would he have reminded Augustus so often of the occasion, adding further insult by calling it a crime?[206] Since each allusion would have been a new offense,[207] it is easier to believe that Augustus would have had Ovid killed.[208] In addition, this theory introduces difficult problems of interpretation: Why does Ovid say the mistake is a wound which grieves Augustus?[209] Why does

he think it important to claim that he received no reward
from his mistake? [210] Does Ovid mean he is procurer for
Augustus? Would Ovid in this context brag of his own
virtuous life and Augustus' failure to exercise censorial
power against him? [211]

Of all sexual deviations attributed to Augustus, the most
sensational would appear to be incest. Sometimes he is alleged to have indulged this unusual taste with his own daughter, in which case the incest must have occurred before she
was exiled. More often the charge concerns his granddaughter, but, at the time the deed is commonly supposed to have
occurred, the emperor was an ailing seventy, his daughter in
exile was about forty, and his granddaughter was twenty—
a combination of ages which by itself is enough to give pause
to prospective recruits to this theory.[212] The Abbé Hancarville offers in confirmation of the incest a cameo engraved,
purportedly, by Apollonius of Sicyon.[213] The engraving represents a man and woman in a very intimate prelude to the
act of love, and Hancarville submits that the persons so depicted are none other than Augustus and his daughter, Julia.
Nevertheless, even granting the antiquity of the engraved
gems, there is still no identification whatsoever—outside of
Hancarville's active imagination [214]—of the characters in the
cameo.

The roots of this idea lie in the statement by Caligula
which Suetonius (*Gai. Calig.* 23) quotes.[215] This notorious
ruler may have wished to be descended from Augustus on
both sides of his family tree, in which event a plebeian uncle
—Agrippa—may not have appealed to him. So the incest of
Augustus and his daughter may be an invention of Caligula's
in order to endow his own mother fully with the "royal"
blood.[216] In the opinion of Rabener,[217] he could also have
made the charge to justify his own habit of incest with his
sisters. It is more likely, though, that Caligula, who was a
close student and admirer of things Egyptian, governed his

relations with his sisters by a desire to imitate the Ptolemaic system of propagating the monarchy through hereditary marriages between brothers and sisters.[218]

Whatever hidden motives impelled Caligula, Suetonius merely reports this statement, giving it no credit,[219] for otherwise he would surely have mentioned it, as was his wont, when he treated the subject of Augustus' immoral life or his punishment of the two Julias; yet he does not refer to it in any way.[220] On the contrary, he praises the continence and chastity of Augustus' later years (*Aug.* 71): "Ex quibus sive criminibus sive maledictis infamiam impudicitiae facillime refutavit et praesentis et posterae vitae castitate." [221] No ancient historian accuses Augustus of incest, though in their writings they have concealed none of his vices.[222] So Caecilius Minutianus Apuleius (#3) is the first writer known to make this charge, and for a time even this text was suspect, because he was a Renaissance writer who was not above manufacturing convenient quotations.[223] Later research, however, has served to show that it may be authentic. But this question need not detain us. Whatever the date of this Apuleius, his source for the charge of incest was probably Suetonius' quotation of Caligula's claim, and the connection with Ovid could easily have suggested itself to a mind seeking a cause for the poet's exile.

If Minutianus is accepted at face value, the sole way to explain the ten-year lag between the exile of Julia and that of Ovid is to transport Ovid and Augustus to Rhegium, or to bring Julia from there to Rome,[224] a feat no one has managed thus far. Also, if Augustus himself corrupted either or both of the Julias, it is doubtful that even he could have brought himself to punish them, or to denounce his daughter in a letter to the senate.[225] Both Julia and Ovid could have blackmailed the emperor in order to stay their sentences. If that was of no avail, they could have revenged themselves by exposing his duplicity to the world,[226] thus making Au-

gustus "populi publicus ore reus." [227] But surely Augustus
was clever enough not to advertise his dereliction by punishing a witness who had had time to spread the story.

Sexual misconduct by Augustus may therefore be excluded. That the emperor was not a continent man was well
known in Rome, and even if his lusts persisted when he was
seventy and in failing health, no adultery in a man reputed
to have seduced the wife of his closest friend, no licentious-
ness in a man whose wife was allegedly accustomed to sup-
ply him with virgins to deflower, would have surprised Rome
or further impaired his reputation. Pederasty, to be sure,
although common, was not commonly approved; but the
position of Augustus could scarcely have been seriously endangered by a charge (Suet. *Caes.* 49) made openly against
Caesar by his victorious troops. Incest, certainly, might
have been the occasion of some scandal, but we have shown
that at the time of Ovid's exile Augustus' daughter cannot
have been, and his granddaughter probably was not, concerned. Less close relationships would not have occasioned
calamitous scandal, since they would have been within the
degree in which marriage would have been technically possible.

The most crucial argument, however, is that Ovid says
that the deed he witnessed was a *culpa* and occasioned sorrow (*dolor*) to Augustus—neither reasonable statements, if
the deed was done by Augustus, unless we assume that he
felt remorse for his act, in which case his repentance would
scarcely be consistent with his obduracy toward Ovid.

VII
See No Evil

DIANA IN BALNEO

Deville, more than any other, champions the hypothesis—founded upon #13 and on Ovid's analogy (T. II, 105): [228]

Inscius Actaeon vidit sine veste Dianam—

that Diana represents Livia, of whose sexagenarian charms Ovid happened to catch a glimpse as she bathed. This chance view then, cost him his freedom to live anywhere except in Tomis—a dear price, indeed, to pay for so doubtful and unintentional a pleasure. This argument wrongly supposes that Ovid was such an intimate of the palace and of the habits of the ruling family that he could wander into their bathing quarters, secure in the expectation that no aristocratic ablutions would be exposed to his profane gaze.[229] Ovid says he saw a crime, an evil; but the practice of bathing was surely not a crime, not even for an empress, in the Roman empire. And no Roman woman was a Candaules' wife to demand that dishonor be cleansed with blood.

Dio (LVIII, 2) provides us with an interesting insight into the Roman outlook on nudity. Some men while naked came into the presence of Livia [230] and were therefore condemned to death, a punishment which would appear to signify that the Roman attitude viewed nudity—if it were an offense—as an injury to the person seeing, not to the person seen. Of course, in this instance, the real charge must have been intentional disrespect, but Livia had the men spared, saying that to chaste eyes naked men were not different from nude

statues, again lending emphasis by her words to the belief
that, for a Roman, the seer, not the seen, suffered whatever
injury might result from offensive nudity.[231] The same argument applies to the hypotheses that it was one of the Julias
whom Ovid had the misfortune to see in the nude.[232] The
notion reeks of the Middle Ages.[233]

LURIDA ACONITA

Did Ovid blunder upon the horrifying preparations of Livia
for the poisoning of Agrippa Postumus? [234] This hypothesis
is probably based upon the danger Agrippa represented to
Tiberius' succession to the Principate, plus the suspicion that
Livia may have poisoned Lucius and Gaius Caesar (Tac.
Ann. I, 3).[235] But Agrippa was not poisoned; he survived
until the death of Augustus and was then executed by one
of the soldiers who guarded him. And if Ovid saw Livia
preparing a poison she did not use, how can he have known
for whom it was intended? Furthermore, though Romans
may not have known the cultural advantages of today's
ubiquitous drugstore, they could, nevertheless, readily pur-
chase poisons from experts who prepared them. Nothing is
more improbable than that Livia would be playing amateur
pharmacist.

VIII

If This Be Treason

AGRIPPA POSTUMUS

The poet's fall from grace has often been traced to an unhappy implication in politics. Some scholars are even convinced that a political mistake on the part of Ovid is the sole motive sufficient to account for the great anger of Augustus.[236] Villenave believed that this was a perfectly reasonable possibility, since—according to his totally unsupported assertion [237]—Ovid was an accepted habitué of the palace.[238] But Ovid would most certainly have used his intimacy with a court faction, had it existed, to gain his pardon. Ovid, so far as he belonged to a faction or coterie at all, was attached to Messalla. Had Maecenas been Ovid's patron, Villenave would have had some basis for argument. But Maecenas, though he was a promoter of all things Augustan, lost favor about 23 B.C. and died in 8 B.C.[239]

One theory [240] links the poet with Agrippa Postumus concerning whom there is little to say. Since he was a son of Agrippa and Julia, his blood-lines gave him more importance than his native talents warranted. He seems to have been an ill-mannered youth, perhaps because he sensed himself ill-fitted for the position to which he was born. Or else his churlish disposition may have been formed, as Frances Norwood suggests, during a childhood spent in the company of household slaves, bereft of his father and deprived of his mother who was at first too busy and then was banished. His primary interests, not unusual in a teen-age boy, were his own physical prowess and sports. In June of A.D.

4, Augustus adopted him along with Tiberius. But his
temper appears to have continued so unruly that he was sent
into exile in A.D. 7 by senatorial decree. Before the news of
Augustus' death was released in A.D. 14, a centurion was
dispatched to murder Agrippa. Whether Augustus himself
gave the order or Tiberius or Livia is not clear, though these
last two are more popular as suspects.

This hypothesis, that Ovid was linked with Agrippa Postumus has three circumstances to support it. The first is that
Ovid, Agrippa, and the younger Julia were all banished
about the same time.[241] Secondly, Ovid wrote some verses to
Fabius Maximus, which can be construed to admit his connection with some sort of political maneuvering concerning
Agrippa.[242] Finally, if Ovid loved Agrippa's mother, the
elder Julia, he would quite possibly be interested in supporting her son's pretensions to the throne.[243]

The opposition to this particular theory submits, first, that
no convincing proof exists for a love affair between Ovid
and the elder Julia,[244] so that, in this respect, Ovid would
have no reason for siding with Agrippa.

In the verses in question the poet addresses the deceased
Paulus Fabius Maximus, close friend of both Augustus and
himself (P. IV, 6. 9–16) : [245]

> Certus eras pro me, Fabiae laus, Maxime, gentis,
>   Numen ad Augustus supplice voce loqui.
> Occidis ante preces, causamque ego, Maxime, mortis
>   (Nec fuero tanti) me reor esse tuae.
> Iam timero nostram cuiquam mandare salutem:
>   Ipsum morte tua concidit auxilium.
> Coeperat Augustus deceptae ignoscere culpae:
>   Spem nostram terras deseruitque simul.

These words are supposed to mean that Ovid had been associated with Fabius in an attempt to restore Agrippa to
favor. The foundation for this interpretation is provided by

a story reported by Tacitus (*Ann*. I, 5): Fabius and Augustus had gone to Planasia on a secret visit which gave promise of reconciliation with Agrippa. Fabius told his wife, Marcia, who in turn informed her friend, the Empress Livia. Fabius, who died soon after, was suspected of taking his own life for thus having betrayed Augustus. And Marcia was heard to blame herself for causing her husband's death. The story occurs only in Tacitus and is classified by him as a rumor. It was invented, probably, as a hindsight interpretation of the deaths of Fabius, Augustus, and Agrippa in rather close succession. But a rumor is poor ground upon which to construct a serious theory.

Némethy even tailored these verses to fit the theory better. For *concidit* he substituted *constitit*, in line fourteen. His choice is good poetically as well as ingenious for his purpose, but totally unnecessary. The traditional reading is quite satisfactory and is a standard Latin construction, as Owen has demonstrated; [246] it has the weight of all manuscripts behind it.

Ovid's words may be understood simply as poetical exaggeration and egotism.[247] His reference implies that Fabius was not involved in the mistake, because if he were and the fact was known, he too would surely have been punished; if the fact was not known, an undetected accomplice would be the last person to intercede.[248] That Ovid considers himself bad luck to all who try to help him—in that sense superstitiously believing himself the cause of Fabius' demise and even of Augustus', who had begun to soften toward him [249] —is a reasonable explanation and needs no change in the text or flimsy rumor for support.

We must, however, digress briefly to notice a possible objection to what we have just said. Ovid's wife was a relative [250] or dependent of Marcia, the wife of Fabius Maximus; she was married to Ovid from Fabius' house to which she returned for protection or companionship when her hus-

band was exiled. She was certainly on intimate terms with
Marcia, and Ovid had long been a friend of Fabius himself
(P. I, 2. 129–150). We would suppose, therefore, that
Fabius would have been one of the first to intercede with
Augustus on behalf of the exiled poet. Yet, by Ovid's own
testimony in the passage quoted above, for more than five
years Fabius made no such effort whatsoever and was only
on the point of speaking to Augustus about the matter when
he died in the middle part of A.D. 14.[251] It may be argued,
therefore, that this long delay, which certainly requires some
explanation, is evidence that Fabius, who appears to have
enjoyed the favor and trust of Augustus throughout this
period, did not think it expedient to act until there was prospect of a reconciliation between Augustus and Agrippa,
thus indicating that there was some connection between
Ovid's case and Agrippa's fortunes. Of course, this is possible, but to make it more than a mere possibility we should
have to show that the explanation suggested by Ovid's own
poems is inadequate. He first addressed Fabius (P. I, 2. 26)
in the fourth winter of his exile, by saying that he feared
lest Fabius be antagonized by the very name of the writer,
and immediately tried to conciliate him by admitting himself to be *poena dignum graviore*. This could, of course, be
explained away as the kind of pretense that might be used
when writing to an accomplice who has escaped detection,
but there is nothing impossible or implausible in the more
natural explanation that Fabius, who as a trusted adviser
of Augustus must be presumed to have shared, or to have
feigned to share, the latter's general view of political and
social questions, did believe that Ovid had been justly punished, and was only moved to compassion by Ovid's vivid
portrayal of his own sufferings. Even if we grant, therefore,
that Fabius did attempt to effect a reconciliation between
Augustus and Agrippa and perished in consequence, there

is nothing to show a connection between Ovid and Agrippa; the assumption of such a connection merely raises gratuitous difficulties.[252]

A different and unusual argument in favor of this theory is advanced by Némethy who discovered that the initial letters of certain lines in P. IV, 6 spell out the name *Postumus*.[253] This is a thrilling verification of his thesis. Furthermore, he states that such an acrostic can nowhere else be found in either the *Tristia* or the *Epistulae*.[254] Notwithstanding, de Jonghe counters Némethy by finding in the same poem the name *Silanus* spelled out, thus supporting an entirely different hypothesis about Ovid's mistake.[255] In neither case do regular patterns of intervals occur between the letters of the names. Also, with little effort other formulae can readily be spelled out by this method—*ne incusa, seposuit opes,* and *nequit Musa* are all acrostics from this same poem. We can also find the additional revelation *necnon Iulia mea* together with the exciting confession *nepos sum eius*. And if the poem were only a little longer, we could doubtless discover what songs the sirens sang!

So tenuous is this whole idea that Ovid was involved with Agrippa that it cannot stand against the impact of Tacitus' statement (*Ann.* I, 3) in which he explicitly exonerates Agrippa of any crime, asserting that his unruly, uncontrollable nature, as well as Livia's ambitions for her son, Tiberius, caused his banishment.

Furthermore, Ovid does not speak or act like a man likely to become enmeshed in the machinations of politics, let alone revolution—a possibility he specifically disclaims in #28 as well as in other poems.[256] As a young man, he declined to enter the senate or to embark on the *cursus honorum* (T. IV, 10. 34–38); he preferred instead the peaceful pursuit of poetry under the inspiration of the Muses (T. IV, 10. 39–40). Since the whole bent and tenor of his life was to avoid the activities and responsibilities of public life,[257] he scarcely seems the type of person to be included in a serious conspiracy.[258]

If there was a conspiracy, why should Ovid alone be punished for it? [259] And what could the conspiracy have been? To replace Augustus with Agrippa?—that would unmistakably be revolution. To make Agrippa Augustus' heir without the latter's consent?—how? Or merely to effect a reconciliation?—that would certainly be no crime. No man can conspire alone, but no one besides Ovid seems to have been apprehended and sentenced for the hypothetical conspiracy. How illogical of Augustus to banish this politically ineffective poet while leaving extremely capable men—enemies of Tiberius—in positions of trust! [260]

Ovid says emphatically that he committed no crime and specifically excludes, along with murder, poisonings, and so forth, all activities of a subversive nature, which makes it most unlikely that he could have taken part in a conspiracy. But if his mistake was to see a crime, it is possible, perhaps, that he chanced to witness something of a conspiratorial nature. But then what happened to the real conspirators? Aside from the difficulty that this is pure conjecture, with no foundation in the records of history, the theory can in no way be related to the condemnation of his poetry.[261]

A very recent hypothesis does cleverly connect the poetry and the *error*.[262] Frances Norwood imagines that the younger Julia used Ovid as a cover for her conspiratorial visits to her brother precisely because the poet's well-known disinclination toward politics would allay Augustus' suspicions. She duped Ovid into acting as her escort on these visits by engaging him to teach her rude brother the civilizing refinements of literature and Ovid used the *Ars amatoria* as his textbook. This hypothesis is carried so far as to suggest that Agrippa's sister may have entered into incestuous relations with her brother in order to bind him closer to the conspiracy in which she, not her mother, was the moving spirit. The younger Julia plotted against her grandfather because she had imbibed revolutionary doctrines from her husband, L. Aemilius Paulus, who was executed, according to this hypothesis, "preferably" in A.D. 6 for conspiring to put Agrippa Postumus on the throne. Next Agrippa was found out toward the end of A.D. 7, Julia between A.D. 7 and 8, and finally Ovid, whose suspicions had been aroused when he saw money or letters change hands between Julia and Agrippa, was banished late in A.D. 8, to silence him. The charges of immorality were mere pretexts to conceal the fact of a conspiracy existing within the imperial family, because Augustus was particularly worried by popular unrest in A.D. 6.

The reconstruction of the affair is ingenious for joining the *Ars amatoria* with the *error* and for linking L. Aemilius Paulus, Julia, Agrippa and Ovid, but it is more notable for its proliferation of conjectures and assumptions precariously supporting one another to this end. Nor is there a satisfactory explanation for the failure to discover and condemn the major figures in the conspiracy who gave Julia the money or letters whose transfer alerted Ovid to the real business going on behind his back. Furthermore, banishment seems a very dubious means for silencing the likes of Julia, Agrippa, and Ovid; also, the punishment of a bumbling dupe remains still unaccountably more severe than that of the alleged principals.

Sivry constructed a remarkable variation on the Agrippa theme [263] by placing Ovid in the seat of a decemvir,[264] an important judge, so that, in the course of his duties, he stumbled upon a terrible crime committed by Agrippa, which he then foolishly reported when he should have discreetly ignored it, and it was for this lack of prudence that Ovid was relegated. But this gratuitous hypothesis comes to grief with its initial and incredible assumption that Ovid, a famous and happy middle-aged poet, unaccountably resumed the political career that he had abandoned twenty-five or thirty years before.

Among other serious objections to Sivry's theory is the fact that Tacitus, as was reported above, specifically says that Agrippa was guilty of no crime. This theory would also place Tiberius and Livia on the side of Ovid; they should have been grateful to him for eliminating Tiberius' most formidable competitor for the throne,[265] and would have been under a moral and political obligation to procure his recall at the earliest possible moment.

L. AEMILIUS PAULUS

Suetonius (*Aug.* 19), in listing a number of men who had plotted against Augustus, includes the name of the husband of the younger Julia, L. Aemilius Paulus, who was consul in A.D. I. Inevitably, the name of Ovid was associated with his as a partner of conspiracy; [266] yet with the best will in the world, not much of a connection can be established. First, there is no way of knowing when this plot was exposed,[267] for the latest *terminus ante quem* which can be figured with the aid of Dio Cassius (LV, 27) is A.D. 6,[268] but this is not certain, and it is still two years before Ovid was relegated. Again, Ovid is insistent that he committed no crime, took part in no conspiracy.

ANONYMOUS PASQUINADE

In a somewhat different direction, a tentative probe by one scholar would father some anonymous political poetry upon Ovid as the cause of his disgrace.[269] Suetonius merely reports the verses as a sample of the lampoons directed against the emperor (*Aug.* 70): [270]

> Cum primum istorum conduxit mensa choragum,
>   Sexque deos vidit Mallia sexque deas,
> Impia dum Phoebi Caesar mendacia ludit,
>   Dum nova divorum cenat adulteria:
> Omnia se a terris tunc numina declinarunt,
>   Fugit et auratos Jupiter ipse thronos.

Because their style and spirit is said to resemble Ovid's own,[271] it is suggested that these are, indeed, Ovid's lines, and that they are the cause of his punishment, for Augustus lacked the kind of humor which could brook criticism in whatever spirit it may have been offered. Not only does this idea, which is as gratuitous as any that is offered in solution of the problem, lack any historical foundation, but it is explicitly contravened both by Seneca's express statement (*De Ben.* III, 27. 1) that no one was endangered by his statements against Augustus and by Ovid's lifelong disinterest in politics.[272] Also embarrassing to this hypothesis is the fact that the lines were written too long before Ovid's banishment.[273] Nor would banishing Ovid have been the needed remedy, unless Augustus intended to deter others from writing lampoons; but then the maximum of publicity would naturally have been sought.

OVID AND GERMANICUS

We have already noted that so many of Ovid's best friends belonged to the circle of intimates who surrounded Germanicus,[274] and we have also remarked on Ovid's praise of Germanicus in his poetry and his appeals to that prince for intercession.[275] Germanicus belonged to that rare breed of man blessed by the gods. He was seemingly endowed with every virtue and men were instinctively attracted to his standard. The army, the senate, the knights, the provinces, the nobility—all felt for him both admiration and devotion because each class saw in him the promise of protection and promotion for its specific interests.[276]

Born in 15 B.C., Germanicus was the son of Tiberius' brother, Drusus, and the younger Antonia. But in A.D. 4 Augustus ordered Tiberius to adopt him as senior to his own son. Germanicus was all that Tiberius was not—popular, charming, beloved, and trusted—seemingly, by all. In his wife, Agrippina, a daughter of Julia and M. Agrippa, he possessed a competent mate whose drive and ambition spurred him on when his own good nature flagged or was distracted by interests that fascinated him more than becoming the titular head of the Roman Empire. Many were shocked by his unexpected death in A.D. 19. The dying Germanicus was certain that he had been poisoned and asked his wife to avenge him. Agrippina was sure that Tiberius had ordered her husband's murder to remove a dangerous rival to his power.

In the eyes of Tiberius and Livia, if we accept the darkest interpretation of their characters, Germanicus was a redoubtable foe to their designs upon the Principate.[277] Accordingly, they distrusted anyone who favored him or was favored by him, and there are men who believe that this is the true reason why Ovid was so swiftly destroyed.[278] Through him, Tiberius and Livia were striking at Germanicus, and Ovid's mistake was to become too closely associated with that prince.

Owen attempts to give substance to this conjecture by citing Ovid's words in P. II, 8. 38 and 44 and P. III, 1. He contends that this timid, fearful appeal to Tiberius and Livia, plus the careful instructions to his wife on how to approach Livia, are motivated by a political fault through which Ovid offended both Tiberius and Livia.[279] Still, these same loci suit equally well the theory that Ovid was somehow mixed up with a crime of Julia's. In that case, too, Livia and Tiberius would be (or would pretend to be) wroth with

Ovid for having a hand in causing a disgrace to the imperial house.[280] Anyway, Ovid's directions to his wife on the course her intercession should take would be justified no matter what the nature of his fault.[281]

Most difficult to understand about this theory is why Tiberius and Livia should single out a political nonentity for persecution while leaving untouched far more formidable foes to their plans. Nor is it reasonable to suppose that Germanicus would have idly watched the fall of a loyal supporter without exerting himself on his behalf. This theory provides no natural tie-in between the mistake and the charge against Ovid's poetry and must assume that Ovid's *error* was a trap set for him by his imperial enemies.

LIVIA'S DYNASTIC AMBITIONS

Livia has already been presented as Ovid's enemy on two counts. In one theory, Ovid was the powerful protector and supporter of Agrippa, or, at any rate, a partisan of his.[282] The other theory showed us Ovid as a protégé of Germanicus.[283] A third pedantic claim has it that Ovid saw some scene or other—perhaps Livia, Tiberius, and Augustus quarreling over the fate of Agrippa, perhaps some action of Livia's which compromised Augustus and Tiberius.[284]

A fourth hypothesis finds in some of Ovid's verses the cause of Livia's and Tiberius' wrath.[285] Some of these lines occur in the *Metamorphoses* (I, 147–148) and are alleged to refer to Livia and Tiberius as murderers. Even though this book of Ovid's was not published until after his relegation,[286] Livia and Tiberius may have heard it in private recitations.[287] But the lines cited are commonplaces in older authors such as Hesiod ("Εργα 130–138, 181–201) and Catullus (64. 379 ff.), whenever they speak of a decline in the morals of the times. Actually, in this book as in all of his poetry, Ovid is most respectful, even flattering, toward the dynasts.[288] Indeed, if this suggestion were valid, Ovid would certainly have amended his poetry or defended it,[289] but he did neither. If it were true, he might not even have been allowed to publish the work.

Other verses have been found in the *Amores,* which are supposed to ridicule Tiberius, but this theory, contrary to fact, presupposes that Corinna has been proved to be the elder Julia,[290] and argues an extraordinarily patient vindictiveness in both Livia and Tiberius.

The basis for all these assumptions is no firmer than their authors' conviction that only a woman could hate so deeply and lastingly that Ovid would never be pardoned. Therefore, the woman must be Livia, and Ovid must have run afoul of the motivating force of her whole life—Tiberius' succession.[291]

In almost complete contrast is another scholar's idea that Ovid's offense was something so petty that Augustus dared not tell the world. Yet his unimportant slip offended Livia, who destroyed Ovid much as Pompadour crushed Maurepas for a witticism at her expense.[292]

Each of these theories has in common the idea that somehow or other Ovid interfered with Livia's plans to see her son, Tiberius, upon the throne,[293] and the variety among them is enough to indicate how strongly guesswork is at play in their formation.

OVID REFUSED TO PROPAGANDIZE

Perhaps reflecting the age in which they live, some scholars place the blame for Ovid's relegation upon his literary independence.[294] In their view, the poet had the misfortune to defy a totalitarian regime which valued literature primarily as a means of propaganda.[295] Consequently, when he refused to hire out his Muse for the purpose of embellishing the deeds and glories of Augustus and his government, Ovid incurred the wrath of the emperor.[296] Their principal evidence for this conclusion lies in the second book of the *Tristia*.[297]

Lines 314 and 338 are selected to show that Ovid conceives his mistake to have been a failure to sing of heroic themes, of Troy, Thebes, Rome, and especially, of Augustus.[298] But this constitutes a violent dislocation of meaning, since the burden of the context is obviously otherwise. Both before and after these lines, Ovid is lamenting that he did not sing of such heroic topics precisely because his verses on love caused his downfall. In other words, the catastrophe was not due to his lack of praise for Caesar but to his singing too well the praises of love.

In this same second book of the *Tristia*, lines 61 to 76 and 557 to 562, Ovid draws attention to his unremitting praise of Augustus in all his works, according to his talent and capacity.[299] He is trying here to win pardon from Augustus who has often been merciful to those who defied and fought him. But Ovid has never fought against him; on the contrary, he has always praised him and his works. Therefore, he deserves pardon and mercy more justly than Augustus' forgiven opponents (T. II, 41–50). It is not too much to assert that not one of the adherents of this theory offers any evidence for his belief, other than the lines discussed immediately above.

MAECENAS

For a time, the blame for Ovid's banishment was laid on Maecenas, who was accused of engineering the sentence out of pique that his name had never been mentioned in Ovid's works.[300] If Augustus was persuaded to punish Ovid for this reason, he would be a poor emperor, indeed; though he did complain to Horace (Suet. *Horatii poetae vita*) that he was not included in the latter's letters. But Augustus' name appears countless times in the works of Ovid and he would have been thankless, indeed, to punish Ovid so cruelly at Maecenas' behest. The coup de grâce to this hypothesis is the insuperable truth that Maecenas died in 8 B.C.,[301] sixteen years prior to Ovid's relegation in A.D. 8.

VARUS

A similar error was made by Masera, when he attributed the disgrace of Ovid to some ill-considered verses in which the poet is alleged to have cast ridicule upon the Roman general, Varus, for suffering complete defeat in the Teutoburger Forest at the hands of Arminius.[302] But Varus did not meet this fate until the year A.D. 9, one year after Ovid was relegated.

All theories which postulate that Ovid was ruined by political activity or by having made himself disliked by powerful political figures must ignore both Ovid's character, which, as we see from all of his poetry before his exile, was marked by an almost ostentatious disinterest in politics, and Ovid's consistent claim that the cause of his exile was a *culpa* that he inadvertently saw.

IX

The Zeitgeist

OVID OUT OF STEP WITH HIS AGE

In recent years there has emerged in the scholarship that concerns itself with Ovid a marked tendency to represent him as a man who suffered primarily for being out of step with his own time. These interpretations, which would have been meaningless a century or two ago, undoubtedly reflect the current vogue of Hegelian thinking in general, which is in turn related to the widespread sentiment that men today are being acted upon by vast social forces which they can neither hope to control nor fully understand. This sentiment particularly shows the influence of various systems of historiography, such as those of Spengler, Frobenius, Egon Friedell, Karl Joël, and many others, attributing major historical changes to forces which, operating with the blind inexorability of biological growth and decay or geological diastrophism and erosion, determine the intellectual and spiritual climate of an age—thus, incidentally, exempting the historian from a more precise inquiry into specific causes. We are not here concerned with either the philosophical validity of such systems of historiography or the accuracy of the descriptions of the Augustan *Zeitgeist* offered by various scholars, but merely with their hypotheses concerning the immediate cause of the relegation of Ovid by Augustus.

This newest species of hypothesis sees the poet's philosophy of life, or *Weltanschauung,* as conflicting violently with the social,[303] political,[304] religious,[305] moral,[306] literary,[307] or general intellectual [308] attitudes of his age. Therefore, he was

overwhelmed by either general disapprobation or by the resentment of the leaders who were the avatars of the *Zeitgeist*
and was accordingly banished from a world in which he
was a misfit.

The scholars who advance these hypotheses appear to
have lost interest in whatever specific offense Ovid may have
committed or simply to have given up hope of discovering
its precise nature. The fault itself really matters little to
them because it cannot, in their estimation, adequately account for the punishment inflicted upon Ovid. Just as the
majority of scholars have recognized that the *Ars amatoria*
merely provided an official pretext for the relegation, so
the new school tacitly or explicitly sees in the secret *error*,
whatever it may have been, merely a second pretext, possibly frivolous in itself but adequate for judicial formality,
for removing Ovid from a society to whose inner or con-
trolling purposes he was spiritually or intellectually opposed.
The true cause, therefore, was an intangible "spirit of the
times."

This new method of attack on the problem of Ovid's
mysterious mistake is necessarily based upon a web of
speculations and summary analyses, often conjectural and
overly subtle, of the mood of contemporary Roman society.
The mood is usually assumed to have been whatever was
conducive to what happened in the next generation or the
next century. This approach is also based on generalizations
that may be no more than casts in the dark. In most instances,
each writer analyzes the "spirit of the times" in terms of its
various aspects or "trends"—political, social, religious, and
so forth. Then Ovid is discovered to have gone counter to
one or more of the prevailing patterns in these vast areas of
human behavior.

Many volumes have been written at one time or another
concerning each of these elements of the Augustan age. The
scholars who have written these books, despite their atten-

tion to detail and their careful documentation, by no means agree among themselves when they sum up the so-called spirit of the times. They do not even agree on the nature of the basic institutions of the Roman state. A small library of books could be collected on the single question whether the government was or was not in reality a "diarchy"—or even on the relative success or failure of the reform represented by the *Lex Papia Poppaea*. Yet, the authors of the recent discussions of Ovid's exile are content to dispose of all these intricate and delicate historical questions in a few paragraphs or pages, often taking for granted the validity of one or another theory that appeals to them. Needless to say, they have not won the assent of the majority of classical scholars. This treatment of the problem may not unjustly be termed a tour-de-force, for it appears to be tailoring the shape of history to fit a theoretical conclusion concerning the opposition between Ovid and the elusively protean *Zeitgeist*.

The work of Hammond is typical of this approach, which is also employed by Marin,[309] D'Elia,[310] Lepore[311] and others. His first step is to construct a groundwork of precedent for Augustus' action in relegating a poet on account of his works. But the instances he uses—worshipers of Bacchus, Greek philosophers and rhetoricians, musicians—are taken from the early Republic and do not ring true as applied to Ovid's case.[312] When he further suggests a connection between the views of the Hellenistic monarchies and their possible influence upon Augustus' actions, in order to justify a theoretical attitude on the emperor's part toward the function of literature in society,[313] it does not seem unfair to call this a very nebulous connection, indeed. Finally, Ovid is considered to have breached the Platonic precept that poetry has a high didactic function for society. Since Augustus may have held dear this doctrine of Plato, he may, presumably, have punished Ovid for violating it.[314] The entire elaboration is a learned tissue of "maybe," "perhaps," and "if" that cannot help but color and vitiate the conclusion. The same is true for each of these treatments which emphasize the interpretation and classification of historical attitudes and movements as the reason for Ovid's relegation.

All these interpretations must in one way or another meet or avoid the obvious difficulty inherent in the fact that political or cultural states usually represent an equilibrium of opposed or at least divergent forces, so that the *Zeitgeist* will seem a most heterogeneous phenomenon unless we restrict its function to inclining the balance in the direction of the future. Marin represents the authors who recognize only an overall tendency. According to his analysis, the basic cause of Ovid's exile was his atheistic and rational view of life that was opposed to the Roman spirit of moral and religious traditionalism, which was rapidly evolving toward monotheism and had already become frankly dogmatic.[315] D'Elia, on the other hand, so emphasizes the conflict in Augustan society that it would be easy to describe his theory superficially as one that postulates that Ovid was exiled for being too much in step with his age. What he means, of course, is that Ovid was the most complete representative of the attitude of political disinterest, social irresponsibility, and self-indulgent individualism that marked the "post–Civil War" generation in Roman society, at least among the upper classes —an attitude that the forces represented by Augustus were determined to suppress. These forces, acting for the preservation of a state menaced by disintegration, attained at least a symbolical triumph when they imprisoned, in the crudest and least refined outpost of the empire, the foremost representative of over-refined aestheticism and sensualism.[316]

The various hypotheses, which we may here group together since their widely divergent arguments all lead to the conclusion that the precise nature of Ovid's blunder is not worth worrying about (for if he had not made it, the *Zeitgeist* would have found some other way of punishing him for his dissent from its purposes), owe much of their impressiveness, we believe, to the fact that they all restate, in fairly complicated terms, a simple truth that no one can possibly doubt. It is obvious that convergent historical forces that we may, if we please, collectively designate as the "spirit of the age," had produced a political and social situation in which Augustus had the power to relegate Ovid to Tomis and to keep him there, on the official pretext that he had encouraged immorality by writing the *Ars amatoria* a decade before he was sentenced. This no one has ever doubted. Ovid went to Tomis and stayed there until his death; there was no revolution—nor, so far as we know, even talk of revolution—in Rome to deliver the poet from the grip of the tyrant. If this be the work of the *Zeitgeist,* then clearly this demipersonification (not too far removed from the Aeons of the Valentinians) is the real cause of Ovid's exile.

We may, however, remark that even complete acceptance of the view that Ovid was relegated by a "spirit" should not discourage efforts to ascertain, if possible, the nature of his secret offense, for a *Zeitgeist* must itself be characterized partly by determination of the limits of its tolerance. It obviously did tolerate, if it did not instigate, the relegation of Ovid, and we must suppose that, since the vast majority of men are never much concerned or interested in the fate of an individual unless they see in it an imminent threat to themselves or an opportunity to advance their own interests, the great majority of the inhabitants of the Roman Empire were quite indifferent to Ovid's misfortune. But the informed circles of Rome, where opinion could and sometimes did modify the structure of the empire, undoubtedly knew by rumor or by accurate report the nature of Ovid's secret offense. They must therefore have regarded his punishment as either an act of autocracy which had perforce to be borne

to avoid greater evils or as a judicial act that was, at least
in part, justified by the nature of the offense. In either case,
therefore, the offense, if it could be determined, would provide one of the most significant indications of what really
was inherent in the "spirit of the age."

X

The Wrath of the Gods

Whatever the explanation, the ancient pagans appear to have been a far more religious people than today's Sunday Christians. Gods and religion were treated as naturally and as intimately as the air the ancients breathed or the food they ate. The Romans, whether in their Republican prime or imperial glory, were no exception.

When Ovid lived, the religious situation was no longer the relatively simple worship of Rome's pristine period. The absorption of the Orient particularly, and of Africa, into Rome's political sphere had also introduced new gods and, by Roman standards, exotic religions, to the Italian ken.

Since religion, unaccountably perhaps to the modern man, did play so large a part in the daily lives of the pagans, it is not unexpected that Ovid's exile should be traced to some kind of taboo he broke or sacrilege he committed in this specially sensitive and sacred area. Specifically, his downfall has been attributed to violations of the mysteries of three different religions as well as to a reputed dabbling in magic and astrology.

The worship of the goddess, Isis, was the most popular religion of the ancient world and was well represented at Rome. This Egyptian export was based upon the story of Osiris, the god of vegetation and of the nether world, who was killed by a rival and torn to pieces. But Isis gathered up his remnants and he was restored to life. Though the religion was abhorred by Augustus and by succeeding emperors for its un-Roman emotionalism and mysticism no less than for its connections with Alexandria and the Ptolemies from whom, through Cleopatra, had come the most serious threat to the nascent Roman empire, it was popular with the masses for its lax morality, its guarantee of redemption, its colorful liturgy, its centuries-old traditions and a clergy that came from a land famed for its mystery. The cult flourished despite continuous official opposition.

A religion more familiar to the Western world of that period and one in which Ovid appears to have shared was that of Eleusis, a small town on the coast, fourteen miles from Athens, which had become the see for the best known non-oracular religion of Greece. The legend of Eleusis was based upon the sorrows and joys of Demeter, goddess of vegetation. Her daughter, Persephone, was abducted by Pluto, king of the underworld. Demeter wandered over the land searching for her and was hospitably received by the people of Eleusis who did not recognize her. She caused a famine to spread over the earth to force Zeus to have her daughter returned. Pluto did restore Persephone, but not before he had tricked her into eating some pomegranate seeds, which act would compel her to return to him in the underworld for part of every year. Demeter and her daughter were joyfully united, and the famine ended abruptly. In gratitude for her kind treatment at Eleusis, Demeter established her religion there, teaching mankind the secrets, presumably, of life and death.

Whatever were the secrets of the mysteries of Eleusis that disappeared when the two-thousand-year-old religion gave way at last to Christianity, this much would seem to be true: the mysteries impressed and expanded the hearts of great men and small, alike, and it is fair to conclude from their two millennia of extreme popularity that they taught men a way of life that made the present more bearable and the future after death more hopeful.

THE MISTAKE: A SACRILEGE
AGAINST ISIS

Ellis, intrigued by the silence of Ovid's contemporaries, concludes that their behavior was motivated by the need of preserving secrecy about sacred mysteries.[317] He finds verification of this conclusion in Ovid's own verses. Especially in the *Ibis,* but also in the *Tristia* and in the *Epistulae ex Ponto,* occur references to shipwrecks and to reopened wounds which seem to reflect some of the doctrines of the Egyptian cult of Isis.[318] For support Ellis calls upon Josephus, who relates how Tiberius banished Mundus for seducing Paulina within the sacred precincts of the temple of Isis.[319] Ellis then ties everything together with the opinion that the younger Julia and Silanus used the temple of Isis as a place of assignation and that Ovid was their confidant.

The starting point of Ellis' argument, however, the supposed silence of Ovid's contemporaries, is, as we have already observed,[320] in all probability merely an illusion produced by the loss of the works in which the subject would have called for mention, including the *De poetis* of Suetonius and all the formal histories of the Augustan age. A shipwreck provides a normal, almost inevitable, metaphor for sudden disaster, as does the reopening of a wound for remembrance of past sorrow, and both images are common in Latin poetry. If Ovid intended these to be specific allusions to an offense such as that which Ellis infers, he would himself have been most tactlessly reopening Augustus' wounds. Also, if the references are, as Ellis assumes, to unmentionable mysteries, Ovid would be guilty of making strong (and *ex hypothesi* intelligible) allusions to something which was supposed to be kept secret.[321] Furthermore, Ellis has misunderstood Ovid's specific references to the cult of Isis, especially (P. I, 1, 51–58): [322]

Vidi ego linigerae numen violasse fatentem
    Isidis Isiacos ante sedere focos.
Alter, ob huic similem privatus lumine culpam,
    Clamabat media se meruisse via.
Talia caelestes fieri praeconia gaudent,
    Ut sua quid valeant numina teste probent.
Saepe levant poenas ereptaque lumina reddunt,
    Cum bene peccati paenituisse vident.

In these lines Ovid speaks of two other persons, not of himself. And he is using analogies, not exact correspondences. He does not argue that he was guilty of a similar crime of sacrilege but that he committed no crime. His mistake was to witness unexpectedly someone else perpetrate a crime. In keeping with this insistence, Ovid, in the lines immediately preceding the quotation above, after an indirect comparison of Augustus to various deities, argues that the fact that he has been punished by Augustus, whether justly or unjustly,[323] does not mean that Augustus will reject his devotion. The quoted passage ends with the pertinent observation that divinities, such as Isis, who have punished, remit the punishments—even restoring eyesight—on evidence of sincere repentance on the part of the sinner. This passage is immediately followed by an emphatic assurance that Ovid has most sincerely repented.[324] The implication is obvious. The choice of Isis as the deity to illustrate Ovid's point was dictated by the fact that, although Ovid could have alluded to Stesichorus and even have found a few dubious parallels to the Palinode, in general the whole concept of penance and the remission of divinely inflicted punishment through the sinner's repentance was foreign to Graeco-Roman religion, and was, in fact, one of the aspects of the Oriental cults, especially that of Isis, which most impressed the Romans of Ovid's day.[325]

The parallel which Ellis finds in the incident reported by Josephus is, in the first place, exceedingly remote. No one, surely, will for a moment suppose that the younger Julia was, like Paulina, a matron of exemplary chastity who could be seduced only by means of an imposture in the name of religion, or that Ovid had such a reputation for piety that he could have enacted the role of the priests whom Tiberius crucified. Mundus was exiled, not for profaning a sanctuary, but for having seduced a chaste woman by a deception that was tantamount to rape, and if he had had Roman accomplices, they would probably also have been exiled, but for the same reason.

In the second place, the incident which Ellis considers a parallel is, if carefully studied, a conclusive refutation of his theory. Not only did the cult of Isis have an unsavory reputation in the more respectable part of Roman society, as is shown, among other things, by the fact that Ovid, ten years before his exile, takes it for granted that temples of Isis, like synagogues, are convenient places of assignation and places where any man can easily find a "pick up," [326] but the cult was regarded with steadfast contempt and hostility by all the conservative elements of Rome and especially by all who shared Augustus' desire to revive the national religion. On five different occasions between 59 and 48 B.C., the senate had ordered the destruction of all altars and statues consecrated to Isis, and the only large temple that we know of in this period was levelled to the ground, so that Cicero (*ad Att.* II, 17, 2) [327] could with satisfaction use its name as a synonym for complete destruction.[328] It is true that the cult was popular with aliens and the rabble, for it was evidently to conciliate these elements that the triumvirs (including, of course, Octavian) promised in 43 B.C. to erect a temple to Isis with public funds. The promise appears, however, not to have been carried out, or, if it was, the temple was again razed when Augustus attained supreme power. In 28 B.C. altars to Isis and Serapis were prohibited within the *pomerium;* seven years later the area within which the prohibition was to be enforced was enlarged.[329] That Augustus had no respect for the Egyptian cults is well known, (Suet. *Aug.* 93),[330] and we are entitled to suppose that he, like Tiberius, merely extended to the alien and outlandish gods a grim toleration as long as their votaries committed no overt act which would provide grounds for more vigorous measures. The desired provocation was given by Mundus' accomplices in A.D. 19. The very thoroughness with which the imperial government proceeded to suppress the obnoxious cults shows that it was trying to extirpate a "focal infection" that it had long wished to excise.[331] In the light of these facts it is clear that Augustus certainly would not have punished any profanation of a temple of Isis.[332] Indeed, given the fact that he did not attempt to conceal the disgrace of either Julia, if his granddaughter's adulteries had been in any way connected with the alien cult, he would probably have acted as drastically as did Tiberius eleven years later.

Ellis vainly seeks to prop up his theory with ancillary arguments of highly implausible subtlety—who, for example, can believe that Augustus selected Tomis as the place of Ovid's exile because the sound of the name suggests a word that had significance in the cult of Isis? His hypothesis, we believe, is one of the flimsiest of all the conjectures that have been taken seriously by scholars.

OVID REVEALED MYSTERIES OF ELEUSIS

There is a theory, developed by Newton, that Ovid unknowingly disclosed some elements of the Eleusinian mysteries in his poetical works.[333] This idea has been cavalierly dismissed by one gentleman as unworthy even of refutation.[334] We must, however, impartially examine it here.

Newton's whole theory hinges upon his postulate that Ovid

wrote of the mysteries without realizing the fact, because he
had never been initiated into them. In Ovid, he finds an
abundance of allusions and references to, and explanations
of, the mysteries of Eleusis.[335] But if Ovid had been initiated
into the mysteries and did not intend to violate their secrecy,
these allusions, references, and explanations must be mere
figments of Newton's imagination.

Ovid does seem to have been an initiate of Eleusis, and
that at an early age. Herrmann believes that he underwent
the initiation during his travels in Greece with Macer.[336] For
in his first great work, Ovid says (*A.A.* II, 601 ff.): [337]

> Quis Cereris ritus ausit vulgare profanis,
>   Magnaque Threïcia sacra reperta Samo?
> Exigua est virtus praestare silentia rebus:
>   At contra gravis est culpa tacenda loqui.

Not only does Newton assert positively, without grounds,
that Ovid was not an initiate, but he necessarily assumes that
Ovid is lying with regard to many details concerning his
mistake. For Ovid says unmistakably that he saw a crime;
that he knew enough to have sought advice, though he did
not do so; that he did something to make him ashamed—
all of which indicates knowledge on Ovid's part of the nature
of his mistake before he was found out.

More surprising still is Newton's belief that the *Ars amatoria* saved Ovid's life, for the *Metamorphoses* were the work
in which the poet gave away the mysteries of Eleusis.[338]
Specifically, *Meta.* XV, 368 ff. contained their secret. It
would follow therefore that if Ovid had not written the *Ars,*
Augustus would have been able to find no pretext to save
him from death.[339] Once more, it has to be recalled that the
Metamorphoses were not published formally at the time of
Ovid's relegation. Ovid would have corrected or amended
them before publication, or the authorities might have completely destroyed them had they been at fault.[340]

Furthermore, there is no evidence from Rome that anyone was ever punished there for revealing a mystery. Newton
claims that the pagans held this crime punishable by death,
but he gives no proof for this statement.[341] He also says that
revealing these mysteries was considered in Rome to be a
crime more serious than forgery or murder.[342] That these
conclusions of his are wholly gratuitous can be easily de-
duced from his own testimony that "not a syllable occurs in
the Roman code on the subject of disclosing the Mysteries." [343] And, as a matter of fact, it is in the Augustan age
that allusions to the nature of the Eleusinian mysteries become so frequent that one scholar, at least, feels that we have
enough material for a complete reconstruction of all essen-
tials [344] and there is no indication that any of these authors
was molested or even approached.

OVID PROFANED THE RITES OF
THE BONA DEA

The Bona Dea was one of those typically ancient Roman
deities about whom we know so little that even her name is
uncertain. She was worshipped exclusively by women and
her major feast was celebrated on a night in December in
the house of a magistrate with *imperium,* either a consul or a
praetor, whose wife presided over the ceremonies with the
help of the vestal virgins. The secrets of her rites evidently
piqued the curiosity of the ancients, since Clodius was indicted for disguising himself as a woman and attempting to
spy on the ceremonies of December 62 B.C., at the home of
Julius Caesar. With such a precedent, the temptation to
compare Ovid's blunder with Clodius' crime was unavoid-
able, and Herrmann, though he disagrees with Newton, also
believes that the poet's fault was religious. He thinks that
Ovid's mistake was to be present illicitly at the ceremonies
in honor of the Bona Dea.[345] In the process, Ovid saw the

Empress Livia in the nude.[346] The better to establish his thesis, Herrmann changes the text, always a hazardous procedure, but never more so than when the accepted text is satisfactory, settled and unquestioned. In the verse (T. III, 5. 49): [347]

> Inscia quod crimen viderunt lumina plector,

Herrmann would change the word *crimen,* attested by all the manuscripts, to *numen,* because this would support his notion that Ovid saw the nude Livia.[348] At the same time, of course, it eliminates the idea that Ovid saw a crime. (Herrmann presumably forgot to amend *culpa* in T. II, 104, although *nuda* could have been hammered into its place, thus absolutely proving his point.)

A further defect in Herrmann's hypothesis is that he must reject Ovid's testimony that the fault was something unpremeditated. For Herrmann no chance was involved: Ovid acted deliberately, with forethought; he intruded upon the rites of the Bona Dea to improve his knowledge of religious practices.[349] He was, in fact, conscientiously conducting research for the last book of the *Fasti,* in which the ceremonies of the Bona Dea would presumably have had to be recorded in the early part of December. He was, therefore, guilty of the same crime as Clodius, although for a far different motive, and like Clodius escaped apprehension at the time, but was seen and, later, denounced. Herrmann, despite the famous trial of Clodius, insists that there was no law which specifically forbade the intrusion of a man into rites from which all males were jealously excluded, so that his hypothesis is not destroyed by Ovid's protestation that he did nothing forbidden by law (P. II, 9. 71): [350]

> Nec quicquam, quod lege vetor committere, feci.

There is much that is preposterous in Herrmann's article, from the strange notion that only one woman was available in Rome to serve as mistress to Ticidas, Memmius, Horace,

Propertius, and Ovid (to say nothing of the claim that she had earlier been the mistress of Cicero's son-in-law, Dolabella!), to an attempt to support his hypothesis by appealing to the poetic intuition which he believes Baudelaire to have displayed in lines which mean just the opposite of what Herrmann supposes.[351] But if we overlook these regrettable vagaries, Herrmann has made a serious contribution to the investigation. His hypothesis, although open to objections, is more plausible than most, and does account more or less satisfactorily for most of the elements of the situation to be inferred from Ovid's poems written in exile—accounts for them, in fact, more thoroughly than Herrmann himself claims in his article.

The theory, to begin with, fully explains the hostility of Livia toward Ovid, for apart from whatever resentment she may personally have felt at his intrusion (whether or not she was nude during the ceremony), the Bona Dea was a deity for whom she felt, or at least expressed, special devotion, having (as Herrmann did not know), restored at her own expense the goddess' temple on the slope of the Aventine.[352] It also accounts for the severity and personal animus of Augustus, for, quite apart from whatever resentment Livia may have felt, the intrusion of a man into Augustus' own home, from which he himself had been temporarily banished by religious necessity, was a personal insult such as even a man who was not master of the world would resent and might avenge. The intrusion was, on the other hand, an open defiance of the whole program to revive the traditional Roman religious cults together with the spirit of awe and veneration that alone can maintain the vitality of a religion—an attempted revival on which Augustus, whatever the motives that we attribute to him, had undoubtedly set his heart, and to which he had devoted a great amount of money, effort, and, we may believe, anxious thought. The theory also accounts for the otherwise curious ineptitude of relegation as a means of ensuring silence on the part of a witness to a secret, for, in a sense, there was no secret. Whatever happened in the mysteries of the Bona Dea was known, at least, to the many women of high social rank who attended the annual ceremonies, and few will be willing to suppose that Roman women were congenitally so discreet and pious that no one of these ever intimated to a husband or lover the nature of the secrets thus entrusted to her.[353] Women—and men—talk, and there is no sanction so dire that it can effectively paralyze a large number of tongues. All the mysteries of antiquity, like the most secret rites of Masons, the Ku Klux Klan, and even more limited groups today, were doubtless known, at least in part, to some who never participated in them, but they do remain *relatively* secret, for the profane *synetoi* who know them transmit them more or less in confidence and do not broadcast them to the whole world. But a celebrated poet, the darling, we may believe, of all drawing rooms and the wit of the age, for whom the gods were but evidence of the folly of mankind, could be counted on to boast of having cleverly seen what no man had seen before,[354] or at least to make the mysteries the material of his irrepressible mockery, and thus to drain a creed of its solemnity, not with a solemn sneer, but with a lightsome, and therefore more deadly, smile at the vagaries of mankind. Ovid was exiled, not to prevent him from revealing some dire political or family secret, but to prevent him from going about Rome and talking about matters which, like sex in Victorian times, should not be talked about in public. Augustus may well have believed—and many modern readers of Ovid's verse would be inclined to agree with him—that the only way to ensure Ovid's silence on such matters, and to prevent the Bona Dea from becoming the subject of conversation and the object of sprightly ridicule in half the salons of Rome, was to confine him to a frontier post so primitive that one could be sure that it had no society at all.

The theory also can be fitted to other facts without twisting them with manifest violence. We know so little about the rites of the Bona Dea [355] that we can readily believe that there was some part of the ritual that came as a surprise to Ovid, so that he could claim, not without some truth, that he had not intended to see it. The ceremonies, whether or not so modified by the influence of an equally obscure Greek cult,[356] were of great antiquity, coeval with, or more ancient than, Rome itself. It is even probable that they contained much that was rustic and naïve, whether or not obscene,[357] that would have seemed fatuous and crude in an age that prided itself on elegance and sophistication and laughed at the Sabinae who were not only virtuous but undeniably *immundae* (*Amores* I, 8. 39).

We could further commend the ingeniousness of Herrmann's solution—and we shall in a moment return to one of its most noteworthy features—but we must observe that there are some facts which cannot be accommodated to it. As we intimated at the beginning of this discussion, we cannot permit Herrmann to rewrite a line by substituting *numen* for *crimen,* although we could perhaps weather that reef by arguing that since *crimen* does not mean "crime," but rather "accusation," Ovid could be using it here by metonymy to mean "subject of accusation," as he does use it elsewhere to mean "object of accusation." [358] The line would thus mean, "I am punished because my unknowing eyes saw the thing that I am accused of seeing." But we need not try to force that meaning on Ovid's words because this would in no way free us from the insurmountable difficulty of such passages as T. II, 104:

> Cur imprudenti cognita culpa mihi?

This must mean, "Why did a fault become known to me when I was unsuspecting?" The blameworthy act must have been another's, not Ovid's. Now the ritual of the Bona Dea, whatever its details, would by definition not be, or contain, a *culpa,* since it was enjoined by *religio,* nor would Ovid, whatever his private opinion, so describe it. The only way, therefore, to save Herrmann's hypothesis *malgré lui* is to suppose that at the particular ceremony that Ovid witnessed something untoward occurred—some episode that was shocking and disgraceful, if not actually criminal—which, given the nature of the ceremony, had to be hushed up. This is not by any means impossible, for it is quite likely that some of the participants in the ceremony, did become inebriated, even if drunkenness was not, as in some Bacchic cults, ritually enjoined, and the chances of misadventure, from an ill-omened mistake in ritual to the accidental death of a vestal or other participant, were therefore present. But this is to suppose a coincidence, and no explanation that assumes an improbable coincidence can be cogent unless it can be shown that there is no alternative to the assumption. Therefore, although we must acknowledge the ingenuity and suggestiveness of Herrmann's theory, we cannot accept it as a valid or probable solution, and we need not ask whether or not Ovid would have undertaken, at his age, a hazardous and difficult masquerade, when he could certainly have obtained a complete account of what happened from whatever woman served as his accomplice in procuring admission, without the risk of finding himself in the embarrassing situation of the Aristophanic Euripides.

Herrmann, however, has the great merit of having first connected with our problem another puzzling fact in Ovid's biography. Ovid clearly and explicitly tells us that he wrote twelve books of *Fasti* before he was exiled (T. II, 549–552): [359]

> Sex ego Fastorum scripsi totidemque libellos,
> Cumque suo finem mense volumen habet,
> Idque tuo nuper scriptum sub nomine, Caesar,
> Et tibi sacratum sors mea rupit opus.

Procrustean efforts to torture the first line, by emendation or exegesis, to make it yield the meaning "six" and so fit our extant manuscripts of the *Fasti,* are unavailing; [360] Ovid says that he had completed, but had not published, the *Fasti* in twelve books which therefore covered the entire year. Since we now have only six books, in a revision obviously begun late in Ovid's exile and never completed, there are four possibilities: (1) Ovid was, if not lying, at least grossly exaggerating—that he had completed, at most, an outline or rough draft, and never finished the last six books, so that there was nothing in his *scrinia* which could have been published by whoever published the first six books after his death in Tomis; [361] (2) Ovid told the truth, but, while retaining a copy of the first six books, destroyed his only copy or copies of the last six before he left Rome—a theory that may find some support in Ovid's statement (T. IV, 10. 63):

Tunc quoque, cum fugerem, quaedam placitura cremavi.[362]

(3) Ovid completed the work, but his literary executors saw fit to suppress the whole of the second half—obviously a possibility, but with no evidence to recommend it; (4) all twelve books were published, but the last six books were lost in much the same way as the greater part of Tacitus' *Historiae* or the missing parts of the many other works that have come to us in mutilated texts. The traditions that the last six books were either destroyed by Christians to check idolatry or survived until the Renaissance in one or more copies which then disappeared, are all open to the gravest suspicions.[363] If the last six books were extant in antiquity, they were quoted or mentioned by no surviving writer, with the possible exception of Servius, whose commentary, *ad Georg.* I. 43, cites "Ovidius in Fastis" as authority for the undoubted fact that the names of the months *Quintilis* and *Sextilis* were changed to *Iulius* and *Augustus*.[364] On this hypothesis, all twelve books were published by Ovid's executors, for it is

inconceivable that an earlier edition could have been put into circulation sometime after Ovid's departure from Rome and yet been unmentioned in the *Tristia* and *Epistulae ex Ponto*.

We need not here attempt to choose from the four possibilities we have outlined, for they all lead us directly to a greater and, in the present connection, more significant puzzle. Our text of the *Fasti* is a revision presumably begun after the death of Augustus, on August 29, A.D. 14, and either abandoned as hopeless by Ovid or left unfinished at the time of his death in A.D. 17 or 18.[365] In other words, Ovid spent almost six years in exile having in his possession at least six books, complete or at least substantially complete, of a great poem which was, or at least could easily be converted into, the kind of religio-patriotic poetry that Augustus appears to have prized most highly; yet, although Ovid during this period writes verse copiously to procure at least alleviation of his plight, forever swinging the censers of shamelessly outrageous flattery before the ailing Jupiter on the Palatine, and even addresses poetic letters to him directly, he made no effort to publish or even to send to Augustus for approval a work of genius that should have been the most powerful of all arguments for his pardon. This extraordinary conduct becomes reasonable, we believe, only if we infer from it that Ovid did not venture to send the *Fasti* to Augustus because the subject was somehow so connected, directly or indirectly, with his secret *error* that the appearance of the poem was far more likely to incense than to placate the mortal *numen*.[366] In other words, Ovid's strange suppression of a major work during the lifetime of Augustus is a datum which should be taken into consideration in any future attempts to solve the riddle of his relegation, and we must recognize that Herrmann, by pointing out this fact, has made a great contribution to the eventual solution for which we may yet hope.

OVID ATTENDED MAGICAL
CEREMONIES

Like every force for good, religion has its dark fringes and
shadow worlds, a dim area in which lurk magic and astrology,
alluring the ignorant and the credulous. In Ovid's day, these
twin brothers of the twilight boasted a large following, despite official displeasure.

In general, the Oriental religions of the empire spread so
widely and proved so popular because their content was
more exalted than the native Greek or Roman religions and
because they claimed to offer *ex opere operato* salvation,
that is, if you correctly performed the proper rituals, results
were guaranteed—the gods had to complete their part of
the bargain. Since the whole universe was considered to be
alive and since gods and heroes were identified with the
planets and stars, which became therefore intelligent beings,
it was not long before astrologers, too, were offering *ex
opere operato* horoscopes. For these heavenly bodies moved
according to unchanging patterns so that their influence upon
earth was predictable—witness tides, seasons, migrations,
and hibernations. If the stars could be plotted accurately,
their influence upon a man's life at any time could be told.

On the other hand, there are, according to religion, grim
gods, demons, who may affect man. So the magician flour-
ishes because he pretends to command them with cabbalistic
rites appropriate to their nature.

Magic, astrology, and religion all appealed to man's in-
tellect and to his emotions. All offered some degree of certainty to the mind while exacting a firm act of faith from the
will. All achieved standing and respectability, though in
different ways. Religion achieved them because, whatever
its defects, it answers to deeply-felt, innate longings in human nature. But astrology, at least in ancient times, won
great adherence, even from the most intelligent persons, be-

cause it was inextricably and, at the time, undetectably, entangled with the accurate and reliable researches of the burgeoning science of astronomy. Similarly, magic wore a concealing cloak of honesty over its hideous deformities because enough of its absurd and silly ritual was compounded of predictable reagents from what was to become the physical sciences such as chemistry and physics. Furthermore, religious authorities then and now encourage willy-nilly the practice of black magic and lend credence to it by admitting the existence of evil spirits who influence man, and by creating ceremonies such as exorcisms to deal with these malignant beings.

We have, therefore, men like Reinach and Carcopino who have wondered whether Ovid's mistake was to become involved in the toils of the magicians or astrologers. Reinach believes that Ovid attended a magical ceremony where the death of Augustus and the succession of Agrippa was predicted. It is true that at this time there was no law against such a practice as divination,[367] but in A.D. 11 Augustus proscribed it by edict throughout the empire.[368] Tiberius made it an act of treason later.[369] Augustus did, in fact, burn many prophetical books (Suet. *Aug.* 31).[370]

Nevertheless, no evidence exists to prove that such a ceremony took place in A.D. 8. Anyway, Ovid appeared not to have a taste for astrology, nor did he believe in magic, so far as can be determined (*Am.* II, 99). Augustus laughed at predictions concerning himself and displayed his open disdain for astrology by publicly telling which were the stars under whose "influence" he had been born (Dio LVI, 23).

As usual, there is disagreement about the interpretation of texts. Ovid says (T. III, 6. 28): [371]

Lumina funesti conscia facta mali.

Reinach believes that this word *funesti* refers to Augustus' death.[372] Herrmann is equally sure that it refers to Ovid, to the effect it had upon his fate.[373] Of course, the deed—for example, a murder—could have been *funestus* for its victim.

Carcopino modifies Reinach's idea slightly. For him, Ovid's error was to attend a ceremony of hydromancy sponsored by neo-Pythagoreans. These latter were not in favor, and one of their leaders, Nigidius Figulus, a learned scholar, was said to have died in exile for his membership in the sect (Dio XLV, 1. 4).[374] In general, the neo-Pythagoreans may have suffered for their beliefs and practices.[375] However, if Ovid associated with them,[376] it is scarcely possible that he was punished because he attended one of their séances. Nor could he claim that he alone suffered for his *error* (P. II, 2. 15). If he had taken part, as a witness, surely those who had officiated at the affair would have been punished more than he.[377] This would be equally true of Reinach's hypothesis which has Ovid as an assistant, or witness, to the divination.

XI
The Unwitting Pawn

There remains to be mentioned an hypothesis which appears not to have been advanced thus far, although it is a fairly obvious possibility. If the *Ars* was merely an official pretext for the exile, then the mysterious *error* must be the crucial question. But if Ovid's *error* consisted, as he says, of witnessing something that he was not supposed to see, then, whatever the nature of the sight that may be conjectured by our most lurid imaginations, the exile, if ordered by a rational man, cannot have been a means of preserving secrecy by removing a witness; for Ovid had already told the full story to at least one friend and, if he is to be believed, the scandal, whatever it was, became generally known in Rome.[378] The exile of Ovid merely served to confirm the story, whatever it was. And if, as Ovid claims, he saw this sight unintentionally and almost accidentally, then no reasonable man could impute to him moral culpability. Besides, though Augustus, given the fact that absolute power invariably makes men the victims of Ate, may have petulantly imposed an unreasonable punishment even weeks after the offense, he is not likely to have persisted, without reasons which seemed to him sufficient, in an injustice which merely served to expose the arbitrary character of his rule.

Granted these considerations, a simple alternative suggests itself: either Augustus acted unreasonably (as, indeed, he may have done, especially if his personal feelings were deeply involved), or else Ovid's *error* was, in itself, merely a private pretext used by Augustus to avoid disclosing the real cause of his animosity against Ovid.

Many of the hypotheses which we have examined postulate incidents which, while inadequate as causes, would have served as adequate pretexts. If, for example, Ovid had witnessed one of Julia's adulteries, the disparity of the punishments meted out to Ovid and Silanus ceases to be an objection, if Augustus merely took advantage of an opportunity to exile a man whom he wished to remove for other reasons, which he was unwilling to avow, assuming that his motivation was so strong that he did not mind the astonishment his harsh treatment of the poet was sure to arouse.

Such reasons may easily be imagined on the basis of what has happened in historical situations: Ovid may have been in possession of information whose significance he did not realize but might perceive as the result of some policy or decision which Augustus contemplated or thought likely; Ovid may have been a member, or have been suspected of being a member, of a conspiracy which Augustus deemed it best to keep under surveillance rather than expose, because proof was wanting or because the identity of some of the principals had eluded his spies; Ovid may have been the friend of someone whom Augustus was determined to ruin by quasi-legal methods, and may have even been in a position to prove that friend's innocence of the contemplated charge; a dozen similar possibilities will suggest themselves to any imagination.

This leads us to a further possibility: Ovid may never have known the real cause of his exile. A victim of the secret policy or suspicions of a despot, he may vainly have lamented at Tomis an *error* that was not only venial, but really irrelevant.

Clearly, the lack of concrete evidence brackets this suggestion with others which are similarly based upon mere guesswork and speculation. We mention it merely because it is a possibility that appears thus far to have been overlooked.

XII
Sum and Substance

We are now in a position to evaluate the available data concerning the relegation of Ovid.

Aside from the poet himself, there are only two sources that can be called ancient. Pseudo Aurelius Victor (#1) correctly reports the official charge against Ovid. The statement made by Sidonius (#2), although uncorroborated, may well be accurate. Medieval scholiasts and modern scholars err in leaping to the conclusion that the *Caesarea puella* must be the elder Julia, and that Sidonius is reporting the cause of exile. The woman to whom he alludes may have been any woman of suitable age connected by birth or marriage with the family of Augustus or else one of his mistresses. The identity of Corinna has no connection with the exile of Ovid, except in so far as there is a purely speculative possibility that if the liaison was known to Augustus and deeply resented by him, he may have felt a rancor which may have influenced him in determining the mode or the severity of the punishment that he imposed.

The medieval scholia (##3–18) are of little value. Although it is conceivable that two of them may be blunders that have an origin in ancient gossip unknown to us,[379] it is probable that all of them are either derived from misunderstandings of Sidonius' allusion or drawn from the same wells of erudition as the linguistic discovery (#11) that Corinna means *cor-urens*.

Since the multifarious hypotheses of modern scholars

would appear to conflict with the testimony of Ovid himself or with the historical circumstances as these can be reconstructed in the light of our knowledge of the history and customs of the Augustan age, we have found them untenable in whole or in part. As a methodological norm, we note that no hypothesis should be predicated on either the emendation of a text that is sound by paleographic and stylistic standards, or on the assumption that Ovid is deceiving the reader by misstating his view of the facts—it being understood, of course, that Ovid's ostentatious servility to Augustus should deceive no one. We cannot prove that Ovid is not lying, but if he is, the problem becomes by definition insoluble and must so remain, unless new and independent evidence should be discovered in a palimpsest, papyrus, or inscription.

Ovid's statements, though intentionally enigmatic, are not inconsistent with one another. The *Ars amatoria* provided the official pretext for his relegation and therefore constituted a charge against which he had to defend himself; by showing its inadequacy, he really focuses attention on his secret *error*. It is not clear whether such statements as *ingenio perii Naso poeta meo* (#45) are to be understood as meaning only that but for the reputation acquired by his amatory verse, he might have been punished less severely—or as implying that the *error* itself was in some way connected with the composition of poetry.

The *error* was something which it was neither easy nor safe to describe (T. III, 6. 27, *nec breve nec tutum*), which Ovid unwisely (#41, *non sapiens*) did through *stultitia* (T. III, 6. 35) and *simplicitas* (T. I, 5. 42), the last word possibly implying gullibility, meaning excessive or uncritical confidence in another. He had not confided his intention to a friend to whom he confided everything else (T. III, 6. 11), but his reproach to another friend, *ut fera vitarem saxa, monendus eram* (P. II, 6. 10), implies that this friend, who condemned him after the event, had known enough, at least, to give him timely advice, had he chosen to do so. It was evidently as a result of this rash act, which might in itself have been forgiven, since Ovid intended no wrong (#42) and sought no advantage for himself (#31), that he, more or less fortuitously (T. III, 6. 27, *casu*) and certainly un-expectedly (#38, *imprudens*) saw something which he de-scribes as a *culpa* (#26), a *crimen* (#39), and most em-phatically of all, a *funestum malum* (T. III, 6. 27). By seeing this, which obviously must have been an act performed by one or more other people, he brought ruin on himself, so that he can say *meum peccatum est oculos habuisse* (#39) and compare himself to Actaeon, who paid with life for a chance and unintended sight of a ferociously virginal god-dess.[380] The consequence of this, however, was that Augustus deemed himself *laesus* (T. IV, 10. 98) and *offensus* (#23) and proceeded to vent his indignation on the author of what Ovid calls his *offensae* and *vulnera*. And it is quite obvious that Ovid believes his punishment to be unmerited, although, in the same spirit in which he calls this clever and ruthless politician a *deus* and a *numen,* he feels from time to time obliged to pretend that he deserved the punishment and even to say that he would have been just as severe had he been judge in his own case (#35). But this transparent hypocrisy, which Ovid even points out by telling us that it is not *fas* to question the decisions of Augustus (T. I, 2. 96), so little comports with his own character that he repeatedly insists that his *peccatum*, whatever it was, *ut non facinus, sic culpa vocanda est* (#26). The whole is merely a demonstration that *difficile est ad eum scribere qui proscribere potest.*[381]

It is clear that when Ovid saw this sight, he was himself unobserved or unrecognized or among people who either did not understand the gravity of the situation or did not dare to interfere with him. (There is nothing to suggest that he was with accomplices or that anyone else was punished.) Obviously, he was not apprehended or arrested on the spot.

Ovid, however, appears to have been frightened, for he calls himself *timidus* (#41), says *aut timor aut error nobis, prius obfuit error* (T. IV, 4. 39), and says quite definitely that if he had not concealed this one secret from his intimate friend, he would have been safe. Clearly Ovid in retrospect believed that some kind of prompt action—what, we know not—would have saved him. Although Ovid does not say so, it is a reasonable conjecture that he went to visit Cotta on Elba because he wanted to absent himself from Rome until the scandal, whatever it was, blew over. We do not know how long a time intervened before the matter came to the attention of Augustus, nor do we know how it became known that Ovid had seen the *funestum malum*.

There is an apparent discrepancy between Ovid's repeated statements that the secret must never be disclosed—that it must be hidden *caeca nocte* (T. III, 6. 32) and must die with him (#21)—and the frequent statement that his offense is everywhere known, that he is *populi publicus ore reus* (T. I, 1. 23), and *causa meae cunctis nimium quoque nota ruinae* (#22). These can, of course, be reconciled by observing the analogy of many contemporary scandals and crimes, which are known to a limited circle and are freely discussed therein but are nevertheless quite successfully kept from the knowledge of the general public. But they can also be reconciled by postulating that the initial indiscretion (presumably Ovid's presence in whatever place he saw the unmentionable sight or, less probably, his association with the persons concerned) was generally known and condemned, while what he there saw was kept an official secret, and hence was known only to the very restricted circle of informed and interested observers from whom few official secrets can ever be kept.

Although the decision to relegate Ovid to Tomis can be explained as an act of mere vindictiveness, since the penalty was nicely calculated to inflict the maximum of mental and

spiritual distress that could be inflicted without forcing the
victim to suicide, the choice of so isolated a spot can also
have been in part suggested by a desire to remove from circulation a witness who could not be murdered or executed
without undesirable publicity. Ovid had evidently kept the
secret, and could doubtless be kept silent for a time by
threats, but Augustus may well have doubted that he would
be permanently discreet. Tomis was a place that no important Roman was ever likely to visit, or, for that matter could
visit without making it obvious that he was going to see Ovid.

It is reasonable to suppose, therefore, that Augustus may
have been acting to protect the perpetrators of whatever
funestum malum Ovid had seen. This would in turn imply
that they were probably members of his own family whom
he was protecting from public scandal, and it is possible that
Ovid gives us a hint of this in the otherwise odd phraseology
of his compliment to Valerius Corvinus Messalinus, who
probably knew the secret (P. II, 2. 21 f.): [382]

> Quaeque tua est pietas in *totum nomen* Iuli,
>   Te laedi, cum *quis* laeditur inde, putas.

If this is so, Augustus appears to have been successful in
keeping the scandal from public knowledge. Or if he did
not succeed in that, if appears to have been lost with the
books which may have recorded it.

We have attempted to present an historical survey and a
critical analysis of the hypotheses which have been formu-
lated about the nature of the mysterious *error* that Ovid committed and for which Augustus in person, toward the end of
the year A.D. 8, presumably after a secret hearing, publicly
sentenced the fastidious poet to a harsh exile in remote and
barbaric Tomis, ostensibly because he had written the *Ars
amatoria* ten years before.

That an *error* which resulted in such serious consequences

to a famous poet should leave so few traces of its exact nature
is strange, indeed, but may be explained either by official
censorship, though there is no extant account in which the
omission of the story is particularly significant, or else by
its inclusion in histories and records now lost to us, in which
Ovid's exile may have been fully explained.

Ovid himself, while lamenting that he had written the
Ars amatoria, obviously considers the poem to be merely an
official pretext for his punishment that was really caused by
a much more serious incident, in which he seems unexpectedly, though not illegally, to have seen a crime committed
by a person, or persons, who were probably connected more
or less intimately with the imperial family. Even this, however, may have been only a pretext, so far as Augustus was
concerned, since it is possible he wished to prevent Ovid
from discovering or revealing some embarrassing or important secret to which he unwittingly held the key, the importance of which he might have realized, had he remained in
Rome.

At any rate, after Ovid's deliberately vague statements on
the subject, extant ancient sources show only a silence that
is first broken about A.D. 450 by two statements, the first of
which merely gives the official reason for the exile, while the
second is dubious both as to meaning and as to source. In
the Middle Ages, a succession of scholiasts whose intrepid
ignorance is often exceeded only by the typically sensational
character or egregious impossibility of their hypotheses, produced solutions based on the idea *"cherchez la femme,"* an
assumption for which the medieval mind appears to have had
a natural predilection, whenever a problem, historical or
literary, arose to baffle its limited attainments and resources
in the field of classical scholarship.

In a later series of hypotheses the vogue is for a political
error, presumably suggested or encouraged by the widespread
political unrest and revolution of nineteenth-century Europe.

Today's intellectual climate appears to foster a new type of hypothesis which finds Ovid's real *error* in an attitude and spirit of rationalism and atheism which clashed fatally with the dominant conservative elements in Roman society.

The numerous hypotheses on this subject thus fall generally into three categories described, but a detailed analysis reveals that some of them are preposterous, others are plausible at first sight, while a few show great ingenuity; yet none is completely satisfactory, since all fail on several important points to satisfy the conditions imposed by Ovid's own testimony, on which, in the circumstances, we must entirely depend.

The many and diverse attempts to solve this mystery have, however, clarified the terms of the problem, its difficulties, and its limits, so that even if new evidence does not become available, it is possible that modern scholarship may eventually devise an hypothesis which will be cogent, even though certainty can never be attained on the basis of our present resources.

APPENDIXES

CHRONOLOGICAL LIST OF HYPOTHESES

IN THE TEXT

(In general, authors are omitted from this list if they merely adopt or express preference for an earlier hypothesis without advancing additional arguments.)

DATE	AUTHOR	HYPOTHESIS	PAGE
1437	Sicco Polenton	Augustus' sexual or religious aberrations	68–73
c. 1450	Pomponius Laetus	Corinna	38–55
1454–1494	Poliziano, Angelo	Corinna	38–55
1480	Accursius Pisanus	Augustus as Phoebus; Pederasty of Augustus; Adultery with Livia	82–83; 69–70; 51–52
c. 1490	Raphael Regius	Corinna	38–55
1517	C. Rhodiginus	Incest of Augustus	70–72
1558	Z. Justipolitanus	*Ars amatoria*	33–36
1579	H. Ciofano	Incest of Augustus	70–72
1664	G. Gyraldus	Incest of Augustus	70–72
1708	Masson	Connection with crime of younger Julia	55–68
1715	Peter Crinitus	*Ars amatoria*	33–36
1721	Fabricius	Corinna, plus unknown act	38–55
1725–1737	Catrou & Rouille	Athenodorus	68–69
1730	Bayle	Augustus weeping, questioning, or torturing	68
1742	Rochefort	Adultery with younger Julia	53
1747	Goujet	Adultery with younger Julia	53
1770	Minelli	Connection with adultery of younger Julia	55–68
1770	Voltaire	Incest of Augustus	70–72
1773	de Sivry, Poinsinet	Report of Agrippa's crime	81–82

DATE	AUTHOR	HYPOTHESIS	PAGE
1774	Tiraboschi	Connected with adultery of younger Julia	55–68
1782	Hancarville	Incest of Augustus with Julia	70–72
1788	Bayeux	Connected with Silanus and younger Julia	55–68
1788	Ouwens	Connected with adultery of elder Julia	47–51
1791	Withof	Agrippa conspiracy	75–82
1798	Scaliger	*Ars amatoria*	33–36
1809	Villenave	Agrippa conspiracy	75–82
1809	Ginguené	Connected with crime of younger Julia	55–68
		Agrippa conspiracy	75–82
1815	Schoell	Agrippa conspiracy	75–82
1821	Newton	Mysteries of Eleusis	100–102
1821	Rosmini	Connected with adultery of younger Julia	55–68
1828	Fournier-Pescay	Agrippa conspiracy	75–82
1830	Cuvillier-Fleury	Connected with crime of younger Julia	55–68
1837	Merkel	Agrippa conspiracy	75–82
1844	Federico	Incest of Augustus	70–72
1847	Schmidt	Connected with crime of younger Julia	55–68
1847	Dyer	Connected with Silanus and younger Julia	55–68
1853	Browne	Connected with younger Julia	55–68
1854	Roth	Agrippa conspiracy	75–82
1859	Deville	Nude Livia in bath	73–74
1859	Munk	Connected with crime of younger Julia	55–68
1865	Anonymous (in Larousse)	Incest	70–72; 66
		Political conspiracy	75–89
1866	Brooks	Nude Livia in bath;	73–74;
		Moral Turpitude	38–68
1867	Boissier	*Ars amatoria*	33–36
1872	Appel	Connected with younger Julia	55–68
1872	Nageotte	Agrippa conspiracy	75–82
1876	Church	Connected with Silanus and younger Julia	55–68
1877	Cruttwell	Connected with conduct of younger Julia	55–68
1878	Munro	Connected with adultery of younger Julia	55–68

DATE	AUTHOR	HYPOTHESIS	PAGE
1880	Minich	*Amores*	46–49; 86
1881	Ellis	Profaned Mysteries of Iris	95–100
1882	Schoemann	*Metamorphoses*	36–37; 85
1883	Simcox	Connected with conduct of younger Julia	55–68
1883	Koerber	Connected with immorality in ruling family	38–75
1885	Sellar	Connected with Silanus and younger Julia	55–68
1888	Huber	Conspiracy of L. Aemilius Paulus	82
1889	Owen	Livia's dynastic ambitions	85–86
1890	Riley	Politics	75–89
1891	Teuffel	Connected with Silanus and younger Julia	55–68
1892	Ehwald	Connected with Silanus and younger Julia	55–68
1896	Riccardi	Connected with younger Julia	55–68
1897	Dessau	Connected with younger Julia	55–68
1897	Cacciabue	Connected with adultery of younger Julia	55–68
1898	Heitler	No propaganda for Augustus	86–87
1900	Ribbeck	Connected with Silanus and younger Julia	55–68
1902	Cocchia	*Ars amatoria*	33–36
1904	Leopold	Connected with Silanus and younger Julia	55–68
1905	Hartmann	*Metamorphoses*	36–37; 85
1907	Meiser	Connected with adultery of younger Julia	55–68
1907	Peter	Connected with affairs of younger Julia	55–68
1909	Plessis	Germanicus	83–85
1910	Pokrowskij	Connected with Silanus and younger Julia	55–68
1910	Cartault	Connected with adultery of younger Julia	55–68
1910	Reinach	Divination	110–112
c. 1912	Pichon	Connected with affairs of younger Julia	55–68
1913	Pohlenz	Connected with affairs of younger Julia	55–68
1913	Magnus	Agrippa conspiracy	75–82

DATE	AUTHOR	HYPOTHESIS	PAGE
1913	Némethy	Agrippa conspiracy	75–82
1920	Smith, K. F.	Insulted Livia	75–82
1921	Ripert	*Ars amatoria*	33–36
1922	Haight	Connected with adultery of younger Julia	55–68
1925	Carcopino	Neo-Pythagorean séance	112
1926	Levy	Germanicus	83–85
1928	Blum	Agrippa conspiracy	75–82
1929	Masera	Ridicule of Varus	88
1930	Trozzi	Incest between Agrippa and younger Julia	66
1930	Klotz	Connected with younger Julia	55–68
1932	Zimmermann	Agrippa conspiracy	75–82
1933	Martini	Connected with Silanus and younger Julia	55–68
1936	Masefield, John	Agrippa conspiracy; Silanus and younger Julia	75–82; 55–68
1936	Garlow	Anonymous Pasquinades	82–83
1936	Rose	Connected with the affairs of younger Julia	55–68
1937	Bickel	Connected with younger Julia	55–68
1938	Battaglia	Connected with younger Julia	55–68
1938	Wright, F. A.	Connected with Silanus and younger Julia in temple of Isis	55–68; 95–100
1938	Herrmann	Mysteries of Bona Dea	102–110
1945	de Jonghe	Connected with Silanus and younger Julia	55–68
1945	Fränkel	Connected with Silanus and younger Julia	55–68
1953	Martinelli, N.	Agrippa conspiracy	75–82
1954	Cary	Connected with younger Julia	55–68
1955	D'Elia	Political and social conditions	89–95
1955	Marót	*Metamorphoses*	36–37; 85
1957	Highet	Connected with younger Julia	55–68
1958	Alexander	Saw younger Julia nude	73–74
1958	Durling	*Ars amatoria*	33–36
1958	Hammond	Violated literary traditions	89–95
1958	Horváth	Saw Livia poisoning Agrippa	74
1958	Lepore	Social conditions and Ovid's individualism	89–95
1958	Marache	No service to politics and morals	89–95
1958	Marin	Violated religious traditions or committed a political error	89–95

DATE	AUTHOR	HYPOTHESIS	PAGE
1958	Marinescu	Connected with Silanus and younger Julia;	55–68;
		Agrippa conspiracy	75-82
1963	Norwood	Agrippa conspiracy	75–82

TRANSLATIONS OF LATIN PASSAGES

ON TEXT PAGES 24–32

1 For he condemned to exile the poet Ovid—also called Naso
—because he wrote three books on the art of love.

2 "And languishing Ovid, famed for his lascivious poems
and banished to Tomi, too much erstwhile the slave of
Caesar's daughter, whom he called by the foreign name of
Corinna."

3 He was also driven into exile because he had witnessed
Augustus in incest.

4 He was charged before Caesar with having taught illicit
loves to Roman matrons in his writings.

5 Indeed, that man, Ibis, had accused Ovid with regard to
Augustus' wife, and similarly with respect to his book on
love. For these reasons he was sent into exile. Others maintain that he refused to cooperate with the empress when
she solicited him and angered by the rejection, she reported
him to her husband.

6 He had been sent into exile by Octavius Caesar on account
of a book he had written on love which had corrupted
Roman matrons; or, as others prefer, because he had seen
Caesar have relations with his wife or with a youth.

7 The cause is threefold: either on account of a book of art
by which he solicited Romans to incest; . . . the second
cause is that he was said by his enemies to have dallied
with Caesar's wife; . . . the third cause was that he saw
Caesar in an unnatural act with a youth.

8 However, the question is why he was sent into exile, and
there are three answers: first, that he slept with Caesar's

wife, Livia; second, that when he was passing through Caesar's porch like one of the household, he saw Caesar having relations with his male lover; . . . the third cause is that he wrote a book on the art of love in which he had instructed young men how to attract matrons by deception. . . .

9 The emperor indeed held him in hatred for this reason— the book on love is meant—and also for many other causes, because he was reported to have slept with his wife, and, besides, he saw him doing some secret deed.

10 Then he wrote some letters to Tiberius' daughter, addressed under a false and fictitious name, Corinna, which were burned for the crime of lese majesty. This is why he deserved exile.

11 Afterward, he loved the emperor's wife, Livia, whom he called by the pseudonym, Corinna, as though she were a "burning heart."

12 He saw the emperor, Caesar, "using" a youth . . . and already Caesar had suspicions about him concerning his wife and hated him for his book on the art of love. . . .

13 Ovid, by reason of the aforementioned book on the art of love and also because the emperor held him in suspicion concerning his wife . . .

14 The three causes of his exile: namely, the book on the art of love, Diana in the bath, Augustus with a youth.

15 Roman matrons, and upright husbands as well, accused him before the emperor, holding against him the vices of his art, and adding that he had with difficulty committed adultery with the queen.

16 Whence the Roman women imagined that he had slept with the wife of Nero.

17 He was, however, cast out into exile on account of certain poems. . . .

18 At last, when he had aroused Augustus' suspicions because he was believed to have loved Julia, under the name of Corinna, he was sent into exile.

19 Though two crimes, a poem and a blunder, have brought me ruin.

20   As I defend thee on this score, would I could on the rest!
      Thou knowest there is another thing that has injured thee
      more.

21   A part, too, might well perish with me, and I wish that,
      since I would veil them, they might be hidden.

22   The cause of my ruin, but too well known to all, must not
      be revealed by evidence of mine.

23   Thou didst thyself, as is fitting, avenge thine own injury.

24   My fault is heavy, but 'tis one which has dared to destroy
      me alone, attempting no greater crime.

25   I have done naught that the law forbids.

26   Whatever that is, though it does not deserve the term
      "crime," yet it should be called a "fault."

27   I was not guilty of murder when I came to Pontus' shores,
      no baneful poison was mixed by my hand; my seal was not
      convicted by a fraudulent tablet of having imprinted on
      the linen a lying mark.

28   My cause is a better one, for none assert that I have fol-
      lowed arms opposed to thee, or hostile power.

29   I never sought to wreck everything by assailing the life of
      Caesar.

30   I have said nothing, divulged nothing in speech, let slip no
      impious words by reason of too much wine.

31   . . . but by that sin sought no reward.

32   On that day when my ruinous mistake ravished me away.

33   And unless a part of my sin were pardonable. . . .

34   As I defend thee on this score, would I could on the rest!

35   From this punishment that I suffer I could myself take away
      naught, were I forced to be the judge of my own deserts.

36   That even the fact of life I hold to be the gift of a god.

37   Wretched me! were it not for the injury caused me by re-
      cent events. . . . These last events ruin me; one blast
      sends to the bottom of the sea the craft that has so many
      times been safe.

38   Why did I see anything? Why did I make my eyes guilty?
      Why was I so thoughtless as to harbor the knowledge of a
      fault?

39 Because my unwitting eyes beheld a crime, I am punished, and 'tis my sin that I possessed eyes.

40 If you should come to know the course of this great evil.

41 No term save "senseless" and "timid" can be applied to me.

42 But no . . . design was connected with my sin.

43 And though my fault is not free from shame.

44 My fault too involves no little madness.

45 Naso, the bard, whose life his wit betrayed.

46 In such wise I would that my "Art," which ruined a master who feared nothing of the kind, had been turned to ashes!

47 Long ago I, too, sinned in that style of composition—thus a fault not new is suffering a new penalty—and I had published verse when thou wert censuring our sins. . . . Thus the writings which in my youth all thoughtless I supposed would harm me not, have harmed me now that I am old. Late and overfull is the vengeance for that early book, distant is the penalty from the time of the sin.

48 This wantonness has caused thee to hate me on account of the arts which thou didst think disturbed unions that all were forbidden to attack. But no brides have learned deceptions through my teaching.

49 That work has already paid its deserved penalty.

50 Have I sinned further? Do not inquire—that my wrongdoing may hide beneath my "Art" alone.

51 You are the chief cause of my exile.

52 Doubtless for this very reason is she fair to me now because she injured me before, when she was indicted with me for a joint crime.

NOTES

NOTES

[1] "If anyone desires to know all my fortunes, he seeks more than the circumstances permit. . . . A part, too, might well perish with me, and I wish that, since I would veil them, they might be hidden." Cf. T. II, 208; III, 6. 32; P. II, 2. 59.

[2] ". . . the ill repute of my sin . . ."

[3] "I wavered between dubious confession and dubious denial. . . ."

[4] ". . . seeing that 'tis possible for my sin, by condoning my original mistake, to lie unnoticed . . ."

[5] S. G. Owen, *Tristium Liber Secundus*. (Oxford: Clarendon Press, 1924), p. 8.; Kirby Flower Smith, *Martial, the Epigrammatist* (Baltimore: Johns Hopkins Press, 1920), p. 43; Owen and Smith appear to believe that the edict of relegation itself was communicated to Ovid on Elba; though they offer no evidence for their opinion.

[6] "Yet when you heard the cause of my disaster, they say you groaned over my mistake."

[7] The alternative, to take *cladis origo* as the equivalent of *culpa*, would mean that Ovid did not confess the truth to Cotta even after he burst into tears, and that Cotta learned the truth later from another source. This seems highly improbable.

[8] Cf. below, p. 27, #19; see also p. 16.

[9] "Thou didst not condemn my deeds through a decree of the senate." We need not consider the probable sarcasm latent in the implication that the senators were merely lackeys at Augustus' orders.

[10] ". . . nor was my exile ordered by a special court."

[11] ". . . thou didst thyself, as is fitting, avenge thine own injury."

[12] ". . . with words of stern invective . . ."

[13] Theodor Mommsen, *Römisches Strafrecht* (Leipzig: Verlag von Duncker & Humblot, 1899), II, p. 587.

[14] Hermann Fränkel, *Ovid: A Poet between Two Worlds* (Berkeley and Los Angeles: University of California Press, 1945), p. 111; Owen, *TLS*, pp. 40 ff.

[15] This may have been a special section of the *Lex Julia de maritandis ordinibus*, enacted in 18 B.C., but was more probably a separate law, enacted at that time or earlier. Augustus may also have had special

powers in his capacity as *Magister Morum,* an office bestowed on him in 19 B.C. for five years and, quite possibly, renewed at the expiration of that term, although we lack specific information on that point. The contents of the *Lex Julia* may be found in CAH (1923–1939), x. pp. 448 ff.

[16] Fränkel, pp. 111, 228; Owen, *TLS,* p. 42. Not surprisingly, this developed into a favored method for tyranny to promote itself.

[17] Theodor Mommsen, *Römisches Staatsrecht* (Leipzig: Verlag von S. Hirzel, 1874), II, 903.

[18] Owen, *TLS,* pp. 41 f.; A. H. M. Jones, *Studies in Roman Government* (New York: Frederick A. Praeger, Inc., 1960), pp. 14, 83 ff.

[19] The transformation of the republican *provocatio ad populum* into the imperial *provocatio ad Caesarem* seems to have been based on the tribunitial power, but it does not appear that a tribune could ever act as a court.

[20] Censors had power to remove a man from senatorial or equestrian status and to stigmatize by a *nota,* but they never had powers of *relegatio.* The strange hypothesis, advanced by H. Wolkmann, "Zur Rechtssprechung im Prinzipat des Augustus," *Münchener Beiträge zur Papyrusforschung und antiken Rechtsgeschichte,* 1935, 184 ff., that the title of *pater patriae* bestowed on Augustus gave him a *patria potestas* over all Roman citizens, so that he may have sent Ovid to Tomis by the procedure by which a Roman father in the early Republic exiled a son to his country estate, has been deservedly ignored by more recent scholars.

[21] S. G. Owen, *P. Ovidi Nasonis Tristium Libri V* (Oxonii: E Typographeo Clarendoniano, 1889), p. xxv.

[22] Owen, *TLS,* p. 46.

[23] *C. Plinii Caecilii Secundi epistulae ad Traianum Imperatorem cum eiusdem responsis,* ed. E. G. Hardy (London: Macmillan and Co., 1889), p. 165. The question of the continued validity of edicts bestowing benefactions on individuals after the death of the emperor who issued them depends primarily on the case submitted to Trajan by the younger Pliny, *Ep.* X, 58 (66), in which a certain Archippus, a philosopher and escaped convict, claims that he was, in effect, pardoned and restored to civic rights by a benefaction bestowed on him by Domitian, and cites a general edict by Nerva in which the latter announces that in the interests of the *securitas omnium* he will act "ut . . . beneficia . . . ante me concessa servarem." Careful consideration of this *edictum* and the letter annexed to it will show that Nerva is reassuring those who fear that the validity of grants from Domitian may be affected, not by the death of the grantor, but by the decree of *damnatio memoriae* passed after his death. In the supplemental letter Nerva says "Cum rerum omnium ordinatio, quae prioribus temporibus incohatae consummatae sunt, observanda sit, tum epistulis etiam Domitiani standum est." The conclusions to be drawn from this document, therefore, are precisely the opposite of those drawn by Hardy and Owen: an emperor's edicts and even the instructions given

by him in a simple *epistula* were not affected by his death and remained in force until they were formally rescinded. This accords, of course, with the spirit of Roman law under the empire, which seems to have made no distinction between edicts affecting individuals and those affecting groups or communities. The latter were, of course, valid in perpetuity, unless specifically revoked. Special privileges granted by Augustus were maintained by Trajan as part of the "constitution," even when they were contrary to his own general policy; see Plin. *Ep.* X, 79 (83) and 84 (88).

[24] Fränkel, p. 228. Perhaps the precedent was set by Tiberius' oath to observe the *acta* of Augustus (Dio LVII, 8. 5), although the exact form of the oath is unknown; cf. Tac. *Ann.* IV, 37. 4.

[25] "While your letter has been on its way, while mine in answer is traversing so many lands and seas, a year has passed." Tomis was, of course, on the extreme frontiers of the empire, and travelers who could carry letters to or from Ovid must have been rare. *Annus* frequently means a long time, not necessarily one year exactly.

[26] "In Scythia I have passed the five years of an Olympiad; the time is now passing to a second lustrum . . . Augustus had begun to pardon the fault I had committed in error; my hopes at once and the world he left desolate. Yet from my distant abode I sent for your reading a poem—such poem as I could, Brutus, about the new god."

[27] ". . . it were fitting that you be restored by Caesar's command. He said this, yes, but, Carus, already the sixth winter sees me banished beneath the icy pole."

[28] "Either the Adriatic saw me writing these words in the midst of his waters, while I shivered in cold December. . . ."

[29] Modern Constantza in the Dobrudja section of Rumania lies on the site of ancient Tomis. Tomis, rather than Tomi, is justified by the practice of the MSS. of the *Tristia* and *Epistulae ex Ponto*. It is also the older form of the name. For the variety of Greek forms, see W. Pape, *Wörterbuch der griechischen Eigennamen*, p. 3, Braunschweig, 1884, s.v. In Latin *Tomi* seems to appear first in Statius (*Silv.* I, 2. 254). P. Mela (2. 2. 5 in *de situ orbis*) uses a Greek plural, *Tomoe*.

[30] Martin Schanz, and Carl Hosius, *Geschichte der römischen Litteratur* (München: C. H. Beck'sche Verlagsbuchhandlung, 1935), II¹, p. 208.

[31] "Now is the sixth summer wearing away which I must pass on the Cimmerian shore among the skin-clad Getae."

[32] Caelius Rhodiginus (*Lectionum antiquarum libri*, XIII, 1 = ed. Coloniae Allobrogum, 1620, p. 859F) quotes Caecilius Minutianus Apuleius to the effect that Ovid's enemy was Corvinus. If there is any basis for this statement in a suspected source (both Caelius and the Minutianus whom he cites have been accused of forgery (see below, note 64), the person in question cannot be the famous M. Valerius Messalla

Corvinus who remained a faithful friend to Ovid and for whom Ovid
composed an epicedium (P. I, 7. 27–30), nor do we know of a Corvinus
who could have been Ovid's enemy (although, of course, we do not
have a record of all the persons who bore a cognomen common in the
gens Valeria). Of the attempts of modern scholars to identify the object
of Ovid's invective (see Ellis' prolegomena to his edition of the *Ibis*,
Oxonii, 1881, pp. xix ff., with an afterthought in *The Journal of Philology*,
XXIV (1895), 180–182, some are preposterous and the best are merely
possible conjectures (see Antonio La Penna in the prolegomena to his
edition of the *Ibis* [Firenze. 1957], xvii–xix).

[33] *Callimachus*, ed. Rudolfus Pfeiffer (Oxonii: 1949–1953), frag.
381–382.

[34] Pfeiffer ad frag. 382: "Ovidius igitur neque repetivit neque in-
terpretatus est Callimachi ἀράς, sed in universum novas collegit." Pfeiffer
rejects, as do most scholars, the Latin verses quoted in the medieval
scholia on the *Ibis* as translations from Callimachus. F. W. Lenz, in his
recent edition of these scholia (Augustae Taurinorum [1956], pp. 116–
118) concurs in this conclusion.

[35] *Ibis* 9: "Quisquis is est—nam nomen adhuc utcumque tacebo."
Ovid, so far as we know, did not carry out the threat in line 643: "post-
modo plura leges et nomen habentia verum."

[36] A. E. Housman, "The Ibis of Ovid," *The Journal of Philology*,
XXXV (1920), 287 ff. Housman's argument is based on three considerations: (1) Ovid's description of his enemy "is much too good to be true.
If one's enemies are of flesh and blood, they do not carry complaisance
so far as to choose the *dies Alliensis* for their birthday and the most in-
eligible spot in Africa for their birthplace." (2) Ovid's "interminable
and inconsistent series" of learned execrations are too literary and arti-
ficial to "show" sincere and lively hatred." (3) Ovid in P. IV, 14. 44,
which must have been written several years later than the *Ibis*, says
"Extat adhuc nemo saucius ore meo." To these objections we may reply
that (1) women did bear children in Africa on the eighteenth of July,
and while we may grant the improbability of the coincidence that Ovid
describes, everyone knows that the writers of invective do not always
verify rumors which they report and sometimes exaggerate, and the most
that we can infer from Ovid's statement is that his enemy was a man
of whom such a description was not *patently* implausible; (2) the fact
that Ovid was demonstrating Callimachean ingenuity in the body of the
poem does not prove that the person whom he mentions in the exordium
and threatens to attack openly in the conclusion did not exist; (3) Ovid
could have said "nemo saucius ore meo" truthfully, if a little disingenuously, since he did not *name* his enemy in the *Ibis* and the enemy had
suffered no harm—and there is the further possibility that, as La Penna
points out (*op. cit.*, p. xii), Ovid may not have published the *Ibis* at all.
These considerations lead us to agree with La Penna (*ibid.*, p. xiii) that
"lo Housman indulga troppo . . . a sottigliezze ipercritiche," and to

agree with Ellis, Lenz (*op. cit.,* pp. xliv f.), La Penna, Fränkel, and others that Ovid's *Ibis* was an attack on a real enemy whose name Ovid thought it prudent to conceal at the time of writing.

[37] "He suffers me not, though banished to the north wind's icy birthplace, to lie hidden in my exile; cruelly he vexes the wounds that crave repose, and shouts my name in all the Forum, nor allows her who is joined to me in the perpetual union of the marriage-bed to weep for her husband's living corpse. And while I embrace the shattered fragments of my bark, he fights to possess my shipwrecked planks; and he who ought to have extinguished the sudden flames seeks plunder like a robber from the midst of the fire. He strives that my exiled old age may lack sustenance: ah! how much worthier is he himself of my distress!"

[38] " 'Tis thy doing that I am not plundered nor stripped bare by those who have attacked the timbers of my wreckage . . . or as the hungry vulture peers about for the possible sight of some unburied corpse, so there was one, treacherous in my bitter fortune, who, hadst thou suffered it, would have come into my wealth. Him thy courage has repelled with the aid of spirited friends whom I can never thank as they deserve."

[39] Schanz-Hosius, II¹, pp. 244 ff.

[40] The latest possible year, A.D. 11 (after which Ovid would no longer have been able to say he had completed the tenth lustrum of his life, as stated in the first line), is the usual date (e.g., La Penna, *op. cit.,* pp. x–xi), assigned on the basis of the assumption that the *Ibis* is the fulfillment of the threat that Ovid makes in T. IV, 9, to use poetry to make infamous throughout the world the enemy whom his absence from Rome prevents him from prosecuting in the courts. But the *Ibis* conceals the man's name and presupposes that its allusions to him will be cryptic for most readers, since it ends with a threat to denounce the man by name in iambics. The threat in T. IV, 9 may therefore refer to the projected iambics.

[41] The passages are collected in Ellis' prolegomena to his edition of the *Ibis;* many of these, however, are uncertain, since it is improbable that Ovid had in prosperity only *one* feigned friend who turned upon him as soon as it seemed safe to do so. What distinguishes "Ibis" is not ordinary malevolence and slander, but his scheme for obtaining part or all of Ovid's property.

[42] "He strives that my exiled old age may lack sustenance. . . . May the gods forbid! of whom the greatest far is he, who would not have my voyage destitute."

[43] V. Ellis, *ad loc.;* La Penna, *ad loc.*

[44] Owen, *TLS,* pp. 46–47; La Penna, p. viii.

[45] Cf. note 37 above. We shall not insist on the possible force of *debuerat* in *Ibis* 19 (quoted above), which would imply that "Ibis" could have effected a reconciliation with Augustus and was under some obligation to do so.

[46] "He suffers me not to lie hidden in my exile; cruelly he vexes the wounds that crave repose. . . ."

[47] ". . . and shouts my name in all the Forum. . . ."

[48] ". . . so there was one, treacherous in my bitter fortune, who, hadst thou suffered it, would have come into my wealth."

[49] The length of time will depend on the dating of the *Ibis;* cf. above, note 36.

[50] The assumption made by some critics that she would not have gone in any case, is gratuitous and unproved.

[51] Fränkel, pp. 115, 229.

[52] Owen, *TLS,* pp. 33–34.

[53] Note the concluding lines of the last poem of the *Epistulae ex Ponto.*

[54] Schanz-Hosius, II¹, p. 207; Walther Kraus, "Ovidius Naso," Pauly-Wissowa-Kroll, XVIII², 1920.

[55] "The cause of my ruin, but too well known to all. . . ."

[56] This is #1 in the list of *testimonia,* brought together below.

[57] Velleius Paterculus' work, of course, is merely an uncritical summary.

[58] Suet. *De poetis,* frag. 30 Reifferscheid = Hieron. *Chronica,* Olymp., 184, 199.

[59] ". . . and Naso too right gladly e'en in Tomi. . . ."

[60] *Ann.* XII, 22. 3, where, in a list of the victims of the younger Agrippina's jealousy, we find "et Calpurnia illustris femina pervertitur [= relegatur], quia formam eius laudaverat princeps, nulla libidine sed fortuito sermone, unde ira Agrippinae citra ultima stetit." The last words may be a reminiscence of Ovid's address to Augustus, T. II, 127, "citra necem tua constitit ira," and it is significant that the phrase is adapted by Tacitus to refer to a *relegatio* that was unjustly inflicted as the result of an event as fortuitous as Ovid claimed his *error* to have been. But here the parallel seems to end.

[61] Schanz-Hosius, III, 1922, pp. 50, 56.

[62] This means, of course, that we really have no independent confirmation of Ovid's statements, which we can criticize only by the standards of internal consistency, human plausibility, and contemporary Roman institutions, so far as the latter are known to us. No one, however, has seriously questioned either the authenticity of the poems written in exile or Ovid's veracity. (Even Ettore Paratore in his disparaging criticism of "L'elegia autobiografica di Ovidio," *Ovidiana,* pp. 353–378, in which he discovers an "assenza totale di un sincero slancio poetico" in Ovid's later poems, does not question the truth of what Ovid says.) Within the limits of discretion imposed by his plight and, doubtless, a desire to present his case in as favorable a light as possible, Ovid, we may believe, reported the truth as he understood it. Indeed, given the purpose of the poems, it would have been folly for him to do otherwise.

[63] *Carmen* XXIII, 157 ff. This poem is assigned to 461–466 by Schanz-Hosius (IV², pp. 45 ff.); it must be earlier than 469 (C. E. Stevens, *Sidonius Apollinaris and His Age* (Oxford: 1933), pp. 108–111.

[64] Salomon Reinach, "Le tombeau d'Ovide," *Revue de Philologie,* XXX (1906), 275 ff. The passage which Caelius cites (*Lectionum antiquarum libri,* XIII. 1 = ed. Coloniae Allobrogum, 1620, p. 859E) is not to be found in the extant fragments of Minutianus Apuleius (ed. Fridericus Osann, Darmstadii, 1826), but is quoted from Caelius by Mai in Osann's preface, pp. xxv–xxvi. It is unnecessary here to review the long controversy over the authenticity and date of the work of Minutianus Apuleius; cf. O. Skutsch, *Classical Quarterly,* XLII (1948), p. 101. Reinach, *loc. cit.,* defends the accuracy of the information concerning Ovid's tomb and the date of his death given in the same passage, but not found elsewhere. Apuleius also identifies Corvinus as the "Ibis" of Ovid—see note 32.

[65] R. B. C. Huygens, *Accessus ad Auctores.* (Collection Latomus Vol. 15) (Berchem-Bruxelles), 1954, p. 30.

[66] Huygens, p. 30.

[67] Müldener, "Zu Ovid," *Philologus.* IX (1854), 578.

[68] Huygens, p. 31.

[69] B. Nogara, "Di alcune vite e commenti medioevali di Ovidio," *Miscellanea Ceriani* (Milano. Ulrico Hoepli, 1910), 423.

[70] Gustav Przychocki, "De Ovidii 'Caesarea puella,'" *Wiener Studien* XXXVI (1915), 340.

[71] *Ibid.,* p. 341.

[72] Nogara, p. 427.

[73] H. S. Sedlmayer, "Beiträge zur Geschichte der Ovidstudien im Mittelalter," *Wiener Studien,* VI (1884), 143.

[74] *Ibid.*

[75] Przychocki, p. 341.

[76] Sedlmayer, p. 143.

[77] *Ibid.,* p. 144.

[78] *Publii Ovidii Nasonis Ibis,* ed. Petrus Burmannus (Amstelodam: Franciscus Changuion, 1727), IV, 3.

[79] Cf. P. II, 9. 75; III, 3. 69–72.

[80] Ernestus Appel, *Quibus de causis Ovidius ab Augusto relegatus est* (Berolini: Typis G. Hickethier, 1872), p. 9.

[81] Theodore J. de Jonghe, *Publii Ovidii Nasonis Tristium Liber IV* (Groningen: de Waal, 1945), p. 12.

[82] Arthur Leslie Wheeler, *Ovid: Tristia, ex Ponto,* The Loeb Classical Library (Cambridge: Harvard University Press, 1959), p. 161

[83] Schanz-Hosius, p. 209.

[84] Enrico Cocchia, "La relegazione di Ovidio a Tomi," *Atti della Reale Accademia di Archeologia, Lettere e Belle Arti,* XXII (1902), 76.

[85] Owen, *TLS,* p. 21.

[86] Rudolph Zimmerman, "Die Ursachen von Ovids Verbannung," *Rheinisches Museum für Philologie*, LXXXI (1932), 266. E. H. Haight, *Italy Old and New*. (New York: E. P. Dutton & Co., 1922), p. 201; L. P. Wilkinson, *Ovid Recalled*. (Cambridge: Cambridge University Press, 1955) p. 300; Owen, *TLS*, p. 24; Wheeler, p. xiii.

[87] Frédéric Plessis, *La poésie latine*. (Paris: Librairie C. Klincksieck, 1909), p. 416. Cocchia, p. 79.

[88] William H. Alexander, "The *Culpa* of Ovid," *The Classical Journal*, Vol. 53 No. 7 (April 1958), p. 319.

[89] *Ovide, Oeuvres Complètes*, Collection des Auteurs Latins, de M. Nisard (Paris: Firmin Didot Frères, 1850), p. xii; the unsigned preface is probably Nisard's. Wilkinson, pp. 310–311; Mart. *Epig.* 11. 20; Pliny *Ep.* V, 3. 5; IV, 14; Mac. *Sat.* II, 4. 21.

[90] T. II, 545; Owen, *TLS*, p. 25.

[91] Mason Hammond, "Plato and Ovid's Exile," *Harvard Studies in Classical Philology*, LXIII (1958), 353. Cf. T. III, 1. 65 ff.; P. I, 1. 5 ff. There is no evidence that he attempted to forbid private possession of copies of the poem or even that he urged Romans not to read it. The former may mean merely that he was prudent enough not to decree what he could not enforce; the latter might be implied in the condemnation of the author. The implication in P. I, 1. 12 that Brutus had removed the *Ars* from his own library is to be taken with the ironic statement that Brutus will doubtless be afraid to accept the letters sent him from Tomis.

[92] Owen, *TLS*, p. 25.

[93] W. Y. Sellar, "Ovid," *The Encyclopaedia Britannica* (9th ed.; New York: Charles Scribner's Sons, 1885), XVIII, 80; H. M. R. Leopold, *Exulum trias* (Gouda: Koch et Knuttel, 1904), pp. 38–39; Hammond, p. 348.

[94] Wilkinson, p. 298.

[95] Maurice W. Avery, "Ovid's Apologia," *CJ*, XXXII (November, 1936), 101.

[96] Edward Kennard Rand, *Ovid & His Influence* (New York: Longmans, Green & Co., 1928), p. 92.

[97] Marót, Karoly, "L'esilio di Ovidio," *Acta Antiqua Academiae Scientiarum Hungaricae*, III (1955), 226.

[98] In *Am.* I. 4 and II. 12 Ovid says that his mistress has a *vir* from whom she must conceal her liaison with Ovid. Although it is true that the word *vir*, unlike *maritus*, could have been used if Ovid's mistress was merely the concubine of the unnamed man, there is nothing in either poem to suggest that she was a concubine rather than a legal wife.

[99] Note, for example, the assurance with which the author of the series of scholia on the *Ibis*, designated as "C" in La Penna's edition, explains the occasion of the poem: "Quidam invidus fuit violator uxoris Ovidii." This is obviously a mere assumption that is not only not supported by the text of the poem, but is actually contradicted by the clear

implication of what Ovid does say about his enemy. The scholiast evidently found the notion so attractive that he did not pause to reflect on its plausibility.

[100] Cf. Schanz-Hosius, IV², pp. 53 ff.

[101] Alfred Klotz, "Sidonius," Pauly-Wissowa-Kroll, Series 2, II, 2237.

[102] Przychocki, p. 341.

[103] "Corinna often helped her Naso to complete a verse."

[104] There is certainly nothing in the extant *Amores* to justify the statement but, after all, Ovid did, for whatever reason, give to his mistress the name of a noted Greek poetess. As has been pointed out by R. P. Oliver ("The First Edition of the *Amores*," *Transactions of the American Philological Association*, LXXVI (1945), p. 214, note 80), Sidonius' assertion may be defended on the basis of either (a) the possibility that the lost first edition of the *Amores* contained a poem in which Ovid explained his choice of the name or represented himself as participating in an amoebaean composition with her, or (b) the interpretation of *versum complevit* in the metaphorical sense that we mention below.

[105] That she was a woman of literary taste and interest is attested by Statius (*Silv.* II, 7), and we must remember that Lucan did address to her, either before or after their marriage and probably in verse, a *iucunda allocutio* now lost (Stat., *ibid.*), so that even this statement is not in itself absolutely incredible.

[106] Cf. note 104 above.

[107] Anonymous, "Réfutation des conjectures de M. Poinsinet de Sivry, sur la cause de l'exil d'Ovide," *Journal Encyclopédique*, Tome VII, Partie I (Octobre, 1773), 143, calls Sidonius first to identify Corinna, while S. R. Minich, "Sulle cagione della relegazione d'Ovidio a Tomi," *Atti del Reale Istituto Veneto di Scienze, Lettere, ed Arti*. Tomo sesto, serie quinta (Novembre, 1879, Ottobre 1880), p. 1140, emphasizes the 450-year lapse between the death of Ovid and the life of Sidonius.

[108] John P. Binsfield, *Observationes Ovidianae criticae* (Bonn: Carl Georgi, 1860), p. 4.

[109] Johann Huber, *Die Ursachen der Verbannung des Ovid* (Stadtamhof: J. K. Mayr, 1887/88), p. 4; Minich, p. 1140 f.

[110] Horace, *C.* III, 14. 10 and III, 22.2, uses this term for women who, though unmarried, are definitely not maidens. Ovid, *Fasti* II, 557, even designates widows thus. Again, Ovid in *Heroides* I, 115, Propertius in III, 13. 21, and Statius in *Silv.* I, 2. 163 describe married women by this name.

[111] For the word *Caesareus, -a, -um,* the *Thesaurus* indicates the meaning *quod Caesaris est*—something, therefore, which somehow or other refers to Caesar. Citations from Ovid, Lucan, Statius, Ausonius, Martial and others are adduced in which this adjective modifies *numen,*

sanguis, penates, nomen, honor, triumphus, mens, pes, vultus, acies, arma, puer, pudor, pons, aula, suboles, tholus, munus, harena. In every instance we find a meaning more or less close to *quod Caesaris est.* In no case do we discover a metaphorical use of the word.

[112] Paulus Marsus is the first to make this suggestion. His life of Ovid may be found in Burmann's edition.

[113] But the only occurrence of the combination *Caesareus puer* (Stat. *Silv.* III, 4. 7) refers to a freedman of Domitian and, as may be seen from Martial's references to the same man (*Epig.* IX, 17–18; note especially the phrase *Ganymedeas comas*), is used with at least a suggestion of the erotic meaning of *puer.* Possibly, then, Sidonius does imply by his *Caesarea puella* what Statius means when he refers to the *amasius* of Domitian as *Caesareus puer.*

[114] Minich, p. 1141.

[115] Cocchia, p. 53.

[116] Kleinfeller, "Ovidius Naso," Pauly-Wissowa-Kroll, IX, 1397; Herrmann, p. 702.

[117] "And many inquire who my Corinna may be."

[118] "Corinna alone knew her Naso."

[119] M. Nisard, p. ix.

[120] Léon Herrmann, "La faute secrète d'Ovide," *Revue Belge de Philologie et d'Histoire,* XVII (1938), 702.

[121] Przychocki, p. 340.

[122] W. Y. Sellar, *The Roman Poets of the Augustan Age* (Oxford: Clarendon Press, 1899), p. 329.

[123] "And most of my work, unreal and fictitious. . . ."

[124] R. P. Oliver, *TAPA,* LXXVI, p. 191 ff.

[125] *Amores* I, 5, 11, 12; II, 6, 7, 8, 11, 12, 13, 14, 17, 19; III, 1, 12.

[126] *Amores* I, 13. 41, 42. In the light of Professor Oliver's article mentioned above, concerning the probable nature and arrangement of the contents of the second edition of the *Amores,* the woman spoken of here need not be Corinna.

[127] M. Cary, *A History of Rome* (London: Macmillan & Co., Ltd., 1954), p. 513.

[128] Thomas Dyer, "On the Cause of Ovid's Exile," *The Classical Museum,* IV (1847), 231–2.

[129] Cocchia, p. 62.

[130] Huber, p. 4.

[131] Edward N. O'Neil, "Cynthia and the Moon," *Classical Philology,* LIII (1958), 1, challenges this rule on the evidence of verses in which the metrical equivalence of the names cited by Apuleius (*Apol.* 10) would be destroyed through the elision of the one name, but not the other.

[132] Owen, *TLS,* p. 20; Cocchia, p. 62.

[133] G. T. Villenave, "Ovide," *Biographie Universelle Ancienne et Moderne,* ed. Michaud, XXXI (1805), 540.

[134] Johann H. Withof, *Kritische Anmerkungen* (Düsseldorf: J. Christ, Dänzer, 1791), I, pp. 132–133.

[135] Achille Deville, *Essai sur l'exil d'Ovide* (Paris: Firmin Didot Frères, Fils et C¹ᵉ, 1859), p. 19.

[136] ". . . made public the scandals of the imperial house."

[137] "When first I read my youthful songs in public, my beard had been cut but once or twice. My genius had been stirred by her who was sung throughout the city, whom I called, not by a real name, Corinna. Much did I write, but what I thought defective I gave in person to the flames for their revision." Cf. Huber, p. 4; Cocchia, pp. 62–63.

[138] Joannes Masson, *P. Ovidii Nasonis Vita* (Amstelodami: apud viduam Joannis Janssonii a Waesberge, 1708), p. 155.

[139] Herrmann, p. 701; Przychocki, pp. 340–341. The equation of Corinna with Julia is still accepted in Sir William Smith's *Dictionary of Greek and Roman Biography and Mythology* (London: 1890), s.v. "Julia," and V. Ussani, Vincenzo, *Storia della letteratura Latina* (Milano: Francesco Vallardi, 1929), p. 381.

[140] Dyer, p. 232.

[141] *Uxore sua* in #5 and in #8 might mean that Augustus played fast and loose with Ovid's wife, on the face of it a not unlikely possibility, since Augustus had a notorious penchant for the wives of other men according to Suet. *Aug.* 69. 71; but, granted the possibility, the emperor would not worry in the least if it became known, precisely because his practice and reputation in this respect were already well known; nor would there have been the slightest reason for exiling an injured husband (Maecenas had set the example of complacency!). Probably, *sua* here is tantamount, in medieval Latin, to *eius. Uxore Neronis* in #15 may possibly refer to Ti. Claudius Nero, Livia's husband from whom Augustus preëmpted her without respect even to the fact that she was pregnant; or the woman intended may be Antonia Minor, wife of Nero Claudius Drusus. If it refers to the elder Julia, wife of Tiberius, the reference to the latter as Nero suggests that the information comes ultimately from an early ancient source, since a reference to the emperor Tiberius as Nero would be extremely improbable after he became *Princeps,* and almost impossible after the reign of Nero; the name "Nero" would, no doubt, cause a medieval scholar to think at once of the notorious emperor, so this does not sound like a scholiast's way of designating Tiberius.

[142] Tac. *Ann.* IV, 74, testifies to this point of Livia's character. Neither he nor the other historians would have spared Livia, were her conduct otherwise, because they were bent upon publicizing any and all weaknesses of the royal family.

[143] Tac., *Ann.* IV, 1. 9; Dio LVII, 22, LVIII, 11.

[144] Suet. *Tiberius* 62; Tac. *Ann.* IV, 1, V, 5.

[145] Among the clumsy fictions of the scholiasts, none perhaps is more characteristic and amusing than that printed in Owen's edition of the *Tristia,* p. lxxxviii, which blandly explains Ovid's praenomen by assuring us that "Publius de publica fama nuncupatur."

[146] Huber, p. 4.

[147] The charge of incest does not appear in an ancient source earlier than the scholium on Juv. VI, 158, which, although mutilated in its published form, clearly says that Agrippa was exiled for incest with Julia. This is scarcely to be accepted against Tacitus' statement (*Ann.* I, 3) that Agrippa was not known to be guilty of any specific misdeed when he was banished.

[148] The scholium on Juv. VI, 158, referred to in the previous note might trace its origin to this possibility that Julia was exiled in the same year as her brother, Agrippa—twenty-one years before she died.

[149] J. J. Hartmann, "De Ovidio poeta commentatio," *Mnemosyne,* XXXIII (1905), 120.

[150] *Ibid.,* p. 120.

[151] Cf. above, p. 33 and note 86.

[152] Dyer, p. 246.

[153] Michael Pokrowskij, "Neue Beiträge zur Charakteristik Ovids," *Philologus,* Supplementband XI (1907–1910), 378; Pierre Fargues, "Ovide, l'homme et le poete," *Revue des Cours et Conférences,* 1re serie, Vol. XLI, No. 1 (Decembre, 1939), p. 209.

[154] Wilkinson, p. 300; Owen, *TLS,* p. 24; Haight, p. 201; Wheeler, p. xiii.

[155] Charles T. Cruttwell, *A History of Roman Literature* (New York: Charles Scribner's Sons, 1877), p. 309; Gaston Boissier, *L'Opposition sous les Césars* (Paris: Librarie Hachette et C^{1e}, 1892), p. 144; A. A. Fleury—Cuvillier, "Ovide," *Revue de Paris,* XVI (1830), 207; Appel, p. 30.

[156] Wilhelm Adolf Schmidt, *Geschichte der Denk- und Glaubensfreiheit* (Berlin: Verlag von Veit and Comp., 1847), p. 51.

[157] E. Martini, *Einleitung zu Ovid* (Brünn: Rohrer, 1933), p. 5; Wilkinson, p. 300; Schmidt, p. 51.

[158] Sellar, *Enc. Brit.,* p. 80.

[159] P. L. Ginguené, "Extrait d'une dissertation italienne sur l'exil d'Ovide," *La Décade Philosophique Littéraire et Politique,* vol. 2 no. 15, p. 348; Deville, p. 33.

[160] Carlo Rosmini, *Vita d'Ovidio Nasone* (Milan: Giuseppe Pogliani, 1821), pp. 103–106. This point is central in an evaluation of the hypothesis concerning Ovid's exile, and we shall return to it in our final chapter.

[161] Suet. *Aug.* 65; Tac. *Ann.* 3. 24; Dio LV, 10; Vel. Paterc. II, 100; Sen. *De ben.* VI, 32.

[162] The natural inference from Suet. *Aug.* 65. 4 ("Ingemiscens proclamare *solebat*") is that Augustus spoke frequently of the two Julias. Seneca (*De ben.* VI, 32. 2) specifically says that long after the punishment of Julia (*interposito tempore*) he *saepe exclamavit* that the disgrace would not have fallen on him had Agrippa or Maecenas been living at the time. All this suggests that Augustus himself could not keep away from the subject.

[163] "I have composed songs of pleasure and love but in such fashion that no scandal has ever touched my name. No husband exists even amid the common people who doubts his fatherhood through sin of mine. I assure you, my character differs from my verse (my life is moral, my Muse is gay), and most of my work, unreal and fictitious, has allowed itself more licence than its author has had. A book is not an evidence of one's soul, but an honorable impulse that presents very many things suited to charm the ear. Else would Accius be cruel, Terence a reveler, or those would be quarrelsome who sing of fierce war?"

[164] George A. Simcox, *A History of Latin Literature* (New York: Harper & Bros., 1883), I, 370; Cuvillier-Fleury, p. 207; Cruttwell, p. 309; Boissier, p. 144; Appel, p. 30.

[165] Émile Thomas, "Sur les causes de l'exil d'Ovide," *Revue de Philologie de Littérature et d'Histoire Anciennes*, XIII (1889), 49–50.

[166] Zimmerman, p. 266.

[167] Cocchia, p. 76.

[168] In the *Annales*—it is true that he was contemplating (III, 24. 4) a history of the Augustan age in which he promised to describe the fates of the other Romans who suffered for their connection with either of the two Julias, but Ovid was certainly an exceptional case, a man more illustrious than Silanus, so some weight must be accorded to the silence of Tacitus at this point in the *Annales*.

[169] "That even the fact of life I hold to be the gift of a god." Cf. T. I, 2. 61; II, 127; III, 3. 36; IV, 8, 40; V, 2. 55, and so forth.

[170] Alexander, pp. 321–322.

[171] Karl Meiser, "Uber Ovids Begnadigungsgesuch," *Sitzungsberichte der philosophisch-philologischen und der historischen Klasse der K. B. Akadamie der Wissenschaften zu München.* (1907), 175.

[172] H. J. Rose, *A Handbook of Latin Literature* (New York: E. P. Dutton & Co., Inc., 1936), p. 326.

[173] Auguste Cartault, "Encore les causes de la rélégation d'Ovide," *Mélanges offerts à M. Émile Chatelain,* ed. Honoré Champion (Paris: Librairie Ancienne, 1910), p. 50.

[174] Appel, p. 28.

[175] Secundus Cacciabue, *De Ovidii relegationis causis* (Alessandria: G. M. Piccone, 1897), p. 12.

[176] "Why did I see anything? Why did I make my eyes guilty?

Why was I so thoughtless as to harbor the knowledge of a fault? Unwitting was Actaeon when he beheld Diana unclothed; none the less he became the prey of his own hounds."

[177] "Folly is the proper name for my crime."

[178] "Even this fault which has ruined me you will say is no crime, if you should come to know the course of this great evil. Either timidity or a mistake—mistake first—has injured me. Ah, let me not remember my fate!"

[179] "With her good daughters Livia for the safety of her son. . . ."

[180] ". . . so thy good sons' wives and their children."

[181] "Add, too, that his daughters-in-law, his loyal granddaughters, the sons of his grandsons. . . ." The critical apparatus of modern editions indicate that all manuscripts have this line in this place, so there is no indication of interpolation from the margin. Some MSS have *neptem* for *neptes,* but a singular would tactlessly exclude Livilla from the *domus Augusta.*

[182] Owen, *TLS,* p. 24.

[183] Thomas, pp. 49–50.

[184] "Why tell of the disloyalty of comrades, of the petted slaves who injured me?"

[185] Eugène Nageotte, *Ovide, sa vie, ses oeuvres,* Mâcon, imprimerie d'Émile Protat, 1872, p. 191.

[186] Herrmann, p. 724; John Henry Newton, Esq., *Three Enigmas* (London: Thomas Hookham. 1821), p. 40.

[187] Cartault, p. 50.

[188] Boissier, p. 143; Dyer, p. 244; Cartault, p. 50.

[189] Wilkinson, p. 299; Owen, *TLS,* p. 25.

[190] Ovid appears to be following strict chronological order in this autobiographical elegy.

[191] "The upright loyalty of comrades could have alleviated my misfortunes, but a treacherous crowd grew rich on my spoils."

[192] "While others would not even seem to know me, there were but two or three of you who aided me when I was cast forth."

[193] "So long as you are secure you will count many friends; if your life becomes clouded you will be alone . . . Whilst I stood upright, my house, well known indeed but courting no honors, found enough to throng it. Yet, as soon as the shock came, all men feared its fall and discreetly turned their backs in common flight."

[194] Nisard, p. xii.

[195] Cacciabue, p. 12.

[196] Herrmann, p. 700.

[197] "Julia with whom he committed incest and for that reason he was relegated by Augustus."

[198] The Agrippa to whom Juvenal refers was, of course, Herodes Agrippa II, and the *incesta soror* was his sister Berenice (Mentioned by

name in line 156), whom the unreflecting scholiast supposes to have been a Ptolemy. Herodes Agrippa's incestuous relations with his sister were notorious in Rome. The two lines following 158 refer to the Sabbath and the custom of not eating pork and strictly designate Palestine as the place where the incest began, although the lines could just possibly be taken as meaning that the persons concerned were Jews.

[199] Pierre Bayle, *Dictionnaire historique et critique* (4th edition; Leiden: Samuel Luchtmans, 1730), III, 563.

[200] Girloamo Tiraboschi, *Storia della letteratura italiana* (Milano: Nicolo Bettoni e Comp., 1833), p. 92.

[201] Rosmini, p. 100.

[202] Villenave, p. 541; Nageotte, p. 185.

[203] Deville, p. 15.

[204] Anonymous, *Réfutation*, p. 145.

[205] Huber, p. 8.

[206] Mario Trozzi, *Ovidio e i suoi tempi* (Catania: Vincenzo Muglia, 1930), p. 206.

[207] Poinsinet de Sivry, "Lettre . . . sur la vraie cause de l'exil d'Ovide," *Mercure de France,* I (Avril, 1773), 184.

[208] Alfred Church, *Ovid* (Philadelphia: J. B. Lippincott Co., 1876), p. 48.

[209] Masson, p. 158.

[210] Minich, p. 1138.

[211] *Ibid.*

[212] Burmann, p. 26.

[213] Pierre F. H. Hancarville, *Monumens de la vie privée des douze Césars*. À Caprées, chez Sebellius, 1782, pp. 37, 213.

[214] Henri Cohen, *Guide de l'amateur de livres agravures du XVIIIe siècle,* par Seymour de Ricci (Paris, 1912), I col. 475.

[215] Appel, p. 16.

[216] Rosmini, p. 95; Boissier, p. 139.

[217] Burmann, p. 26.

[218] H. P. L'Orange, "Das Geburtsritual der Pharaonen am römischen Kaiserhof," *Symbolae Osloenses,* XXI (1941), 115.

[219] Indeed, the passage clearly implies that Suetonius dismissed the story as an invention of Caligula's.

[220] Bayle, p. 562.

[221] "Of these charges or slanders (whichever we may call them) he easily refuted that for unnatural vice by the purity of his life at the time and afterward." It is true that Suetonius is here referring to banquets at which the guests were said to enact the sexual relations of the twelve gods, and later admits that Augustus was lascivious, had many concubines, and in his later years had a preference for virgins.

[222] Anonymous, *Réfutation,* etc., p. 144.

[223] Paul Lehman, *Pseudo-Antike Literatur des Mittelalters* (Studien

der Bibliothek Warburg, Vol. 13), (Leipzig: B. G. Teubner, 1927), p. 17; Herrmann, p. 699; Cruttwell, pp. 434 ff.

[224] Reinach, "Le Tombeau d'Ovide," pp. 275 ff. Cf. (#3), note.

[225] Dyer, p. 235; Anon., *Réfutation*, etc., p. 144.

[226] Deville, p. 25; Burmann, p. 26.

[227] T. I, 1, 23: "A public criminal by the people's voice."

[228] "Unwitting was Actaeon when he beheld Diana unclothed."

[229] Cocchia, p. 10; Owen, *TLS*, p. 20.

[230] Whether by accident or design is not clear; Dio simply says 'ἀπαντήσαντας αὐτῇ.

[231] The story of Actaeon as told by Ovid (*Meta.* III, 138–252) really supports this view; Diana, acting with the capriciousness of absolute power, resents the intrusion of a mortal as an offense to her dignity and acts to prevent the possibility that he may boast of intimacy with her. The question of what is socially proper in a society is, of course, quite another matter and varies with class. The rule of etiquette stated by Cicero (*De officiis* I, 35, 129), "cum parentibus puberes filii, cum soceris generi non lavantur," for example, if based on a distinction of age, cannot have applied in the public baths.

[232] Deville *et al.;* cf. the chronological list of hypotheses, below.

[233] Augusto Rostagni, *Ibis* (Firenze: Felice le Monnier, 1920), p. 75.

[234] I. K. Horváth, "Impius Aeneas," *Acta Antiqua Academiae Scientiarum Hungaricae*, VI (1958), 385 ff.

[235] Georg Schoemann, "Eine Muthmassung über den wahren Grund von Ovids Relegation," *Philologus*, XLI (1882), 173.

[236] Trozzi, p. 204.

[237] Wilkinson, p. 294; Wheeler, p. xv.

[238] Villenave, p. 541. Villenave's argument is a bit colored by the presence in the back of his mind of a picture of the French court of the eighteenth century.

[239] Wilkinson, p. 294.

[240] Fournier-Pescay, "Ovide," *Biografia universale* (Venezia, G. Molinari, 1828), XLII, 135.

[241] Nisard, p. 12; Trozzi, p. 211; but cf. above, pp. 56–57.

[242] Rudolphus Merkelius, *P. Ovidii Nasonis Tristium Libri quinque et Ibis.* (Berolini: Sumptibus G. Reimeri, 1837), p. 392; Geyza Némethy, *Supplementum Commentariorum ad Ovidii Amores Tristia et Epistulas ex Ponto.* (Budapestini: sumptibus Academiae Litterarum Hungaricae, 1922), p. 44; Émile Ripert, *Ovide, poète de l'amour, des dieux et de l'exile* (Paris: Librairie Armand Colin, 1921), p. 183; Withof, p. 143.

[243] François Voltaire, *Questions sur l'Encyclopédie* (Paris: 1770), II, 237.

[244] We have dealt with this point in Chapter IV.

[245] "Thou, Maximus, glory of the Fabian race, hadst resolved to

appeal for me to the deity of Augustus with the voice of a suppliant. Thou didst die before the prayer was uttered, and I count myself, Maximus—though I am not worth so much—the cause of thy death. Now I fear to entrust my salvation to any; help itself has perished with thy death. Augustus had begun to pardon the fault I committed in error; my hopes at once and the world he left desolate."

[246] Owen, *TLS,* p. 30.

[247] Dyer, p. 242; de Jonghe, p. 9; Herrmann, p. 707; Owen, *TLS,* p. 31.

[248] Unless, of course, the political situation had so changed that he, like Clausewitz after the retreat of Napoleon from Moscow, could show that he had anticipated what was now obviously the correct policy. But we have no reason to believe that any such change of policy took place in the last year of Augustus' life. If it had, Ovid's pardon would have been a matter of course.

[249] Herrmann, p. 707.

[250] Owen's argument (*TLS,* p. 29, n. 5) that Ovid's wife was not a "relation" misses the point. The fact, of which he makes much, that Ovid (who is addressing Fabius) says that his wife came "de vestra domo," not "de vestra gente," means nothing because (quite aside from the possibility of metrical convenience) Ovid could not have said *de vestra gente* for the obvious reason that Fabius and Marcia, given the great rarity of confarreate marriages at that time, almost certainly did not belong to the same *gens.* If Ovid's wife had been related by blood to Fabius, Ovid could, of course, have said *de gente tua,* but if she was related by blood to Marcia, Ovid had no alternative to the expression which he did use except *de gente uxoris tuae,* which would have been both ungracious in a letter addressed to Fabius and inadequate as an expression of what Ovid wants to emphasize, which is simply that his wife was married from Fabius' house. It is entirely possible, therefore, that Ovid's wife was related by blood to Marcia, or to either Marcia or Fabius by any relationship that would not make her a member of the *Gens Fabia.* Ovid implies that she has a real claim on either Marcia or Fabius, such as would result if one of them was her closest surviving relative, when he reminds them that they cannot deny the tie: "non potes hanc salva dissimulare fide."

[251] Fabius must have died between May 14th, when he voted for the coöption of Drusus into the Arval Brotherhood (C. I. L. VI. 2023a = Dessau, 5026), and August 19th, when Augustus himself died.

[252] We should, of course, have to postulate that at the time of Ovid's exile Fabius belonged to the party opposed to Agrippa Postumus, but changed sides in A.D. 14. And if we assume, as proponents of this theory do, that Ovid in Tomis heard the rumor reported by Tacitus that Fabius was hustled untimely from this world or forced to commit suicide because of his efforts on behalf of Agrippa, then Ovid, when he says

reor me esse causam mortis, must mean that it was he who converted Fabius to Agrippa's cause.

[253] Némethy, p. 44.

[254] *Ibid.,* p. 46.

[255] de Jonghe, p. 10.

[256] T. I, 5. 41; III, 5. 45; P. I, 1. 26.

[257] Smith, p. 45. Cf. Fränkel, p. 228; Marót, p. 224; Wilkinson, p. 299.

[258] Sellar, *Encyc. Brit.,* Vol. XVIII, p. 80.

[259] de Jonghe, p. 11.

[260] Fleury, p. 206.

[261] Fargues, p. 212.

[262] Frances Norwood, "The Riddle of Ovid's 'Relegatio,' " *Classical Philology,* LVIII, No. 3 (July, 1963), pp. 150–163.

[263] de Sivry, p. 184.

[264] Ovid, of course, had been either a *triumvir capitalis* or a *decemvir stlitibus iudicandis* at the beginning of his career, but no biographical detail can be more certain than that he withdrew from such offices while a very young man. Cf. T. IV, 10. 33 ff.

[265] Fournier-Pescay, p. 139

[266] Huber, pp. 21 ff.

[267] de Jonghe, p. 9.

[268] R. Ehwald, "Jahresbericht über Ovid vom Juli 1886 bis Dezember 1893," *Jahresbericht über die Fortschritte der classischen Altertumswissenschaft,* LXXX (1895), 8.

[269] Lou W. Garlow, "A Guess As to Why Ovid Was Exiled," *CJ,* XXXII, No. 2 (November, 1936), pp. 103–105.

[270] "As soon as that table of rascals had secured a choragus and Mallia saw six gods and six goddesses, while Caesar impiously plays the false role of Apollo and feasts amid novel debaucheries of the gods; then all the deities turned their faces from the earth and Jupiter himself fled from his golden throne."

[271] Garlow, p. 104.

[272] Cf. above, p. 79–80.

[273] W. Kraus, "Ovidius Naso," Pauly-Wissowa-Kroll, 1917, 40.

[274] de Jonghe, p. 10; Nageotte, p. 187; Plessis, p. 417; Owen, *TLS,* pp. 33–34.

[275] Friedrich Levy, Review of "P. Ovidi Nasonis Tristium Liber Secundus," by S. G. Owen, *Gnomon,* II (1926), 272; Plessis, pp. 417–418; Owen, *TLS,* p. 34.

[276] Salvatore D'Elia, "L'esilio di Ovidio e alcuni aspetti della storia augustea," *Annali della facolta di lettere e di filosofia,* Universita di Napoli, 5 (1955), 156.

[277] Nageotte, p. 187; Plessis, p. 418.

[278] Levy, p. 272.

[279] Owen, *TLS*, pp. 31, 34.

[280] de Jonghe, p. 10.

[281] *Ibid.*, pp. 10–11.

[282] J. P. Charpentier, "Sur Ovide," *Oeuvres complètes d'Ovide,* Bibliothèque Latine-Française, I (Paris: C. L. F. Pankoucke, 1834), xiv.

[283] Villenave, p. 541.

[284] Friedrich Lenz, "Ovid. Bericht über das Schrifttum der Jahre 1928–1937," *Jahresbericht über die Fortschritte der classischen Altertumswissenschaft,* 264 (1939), p. 55.

[285] Schoemann, pp. 172–175; Hartmann, p. 124.

[286] T. I, 7. 37; II, 555; III, 14. 22 ff.

[287] Schoemann, p. 174.

[288] Alexander Riese, "Jahresbericht über die Litteratur zu Ovid aus den Jahren 1880 und 1881," *Jahresbericht über die Fortschritte der classischen Altertumswissenschaft.* XXVII (1883), 73.

[289] Cocchia, p. 50.

[290] Minich, pp. 1153–1156.

[291] Ripert, pp. 179–180.

[292] Smith, p. 45.

[293] T. E. Wright, "The Augustan Poets," *Fifty Years of Classical Scholarship,* ed. Maurice Platnauer (Oxford: Basil Blackwell, 1954), p. 320; Ripert, p. 180; Owen, *TLS*, p. 35.

[294] Brooks Otis, "Ovid and the Augustans," *Transactions and Proceedings of the American Philological Association,* LXIX (1938), 211.

[295] Levy, p. 270.

[296] Moriz Heitler, *Ovids Verbannung.* (Wien: Moritz Perles, 1898), pp. 3, 34.

[297] *Ibid.*, p. 35.

[298] Heitler, pp. 35–36.

[299] Cocchia, p. 47.

[300] Villenave, p. 540.

[301] Vel. Paterc. II, 88; Dio XLIX–LV.

[302] Martini, pp. 7 ff.

[303] D'Elia, pp. 95 ff.

[304] *Ibid.*

[305] Demetrio Marin, "Intorno alle cause dell' esilio di Ovidio," *Ovidiana. Recherches sur Ovide,* ed. N. I. Herescu (Paris: Société d'Edition "Les Belles Lettres," 1958), pp. 406 ff.

[306] Marót, pp. 223 ff.

[307] Hammond, pp. 347 ff.

[308] Ettore Lepore, "Da Cicerone a Ovidio," *La Parola del Passato,* 69–70 (1958), 128 ff.

[309] Marin, p. 406 ff.

[310] D'Elia, pp. 95 ff.

[311] Lepore, pp. 128 ff.

[312] Hammond, p. 349.

[313] *Ibid.*, p. 350.

[314] *Ibid.*, pp. 350–351.

[315] Marin, pp. 407 ff.

[316] D'Elia, pp. 96–98, 144–157.

[317] R. Ellis, *P. Ovidii Nasonis Ibis* (Oxonii: e typographeo Clarendoniano, 1881), p. xxviii.

[318] *Ibid.*, pp. xxix–xxx.

[319] Josephus, *Antiq.* XVIII, 3.

[320] Above, pp. 21 ff.

[321] Cocchia, p. 90; Owen, *TLS,* p. 24.

[322] "I have seen one who confessed to have outraged the deity of linen-wearing Isis sitting before Isis's shrine. Another bereft of sight for a like cause was crying out in the midst of the street that he had deserved it. The gods rejoice in such heraldings that witnesses may attest to their power. Often do they mitigate penalties and restore the sight they have taken away when they behold sincere repentance for sin."

[323] Line 49: "vel merui vel sensi principis iram" ("I have earned or felt the prince's wrath").

[324] Lines 59–60; "Paenitet, o! si quid miserorum creditur ulli, paenitet, et facto torqueor ipse meo" ("I, too, repent! O, if any wretched man is believed in anything, I, too, repent! I feel the torture of my own deed").

[325] Franz Cumont, *The Oriental Religions in Roman Paganism* (New York, 1956 [= 1911]), pp. 40–42, 91–92, 222.

[326] *A.A.* I, 77–78: "nec fuge linigerae Memphitica templa iuvencae: multas illa facit, quod fuit ipsa Iovi."

[327] Isis for Phocis: cf. *R.E.* V⁴, 1902, p. 293.

[328] O. Seeck, "Zur Geschichte des Isiskultus in Rom," *Hermes,* XLIII (1908), 642 ff.; Horst R. Moehring, "The Persecution of the Jews and the Adherents of the Isis Cult at Rome," *Novum Testamentum,* III (1959), 293 ff.; Cumont, *op. cit.*, pp. 82 f.

[329] In addition to the works cited in the preceding note, see G. Wissowa, *Religion und Kultus der Römer* (München, 1902), pp. 292 f.

[330] Herrmann, p. 713; Fargues, p. 211.

[331] Joseph. *Antiq.* XVIII, 66–80 (who can probably be relied on for the main facts in the story of Mundus and Paulina, although he has clearly colored some of the details for contrast with a story which he later distorts or invents for propagandistic purposes; see Moehring's analysis, *op. cit.*); Tac. *Ann.* II, 85. 5; Suet. *Tib.* 36; Dio, XL, 47. 3, XLII, 26. 5. Note the detail, given by Suetonius, that adherents, that is, presumably Roman citizens who had become converts to the superstitions against which action was taken, were compelled (presumably on pain of exile if they refused) to burn their sacred robes and utensils.

[332] Ripert, p. 174.

[333] Newton, p. 14.

[334] Villenave, p. 541.

[335] Newton, pp. 15 ff.

[336] Herrmann, p. 713; cf. P. II, 10. 10 ff.

[337] "Who would dare to publish to the profane the rites of Ceres or the great ceremonies devised in Samothrace? Keeping silence is but a small virtue, but to speak what should not be uttered is a heinous crime."

[338] Newton, pp. 19 ff.

[339] *Ibid.*, p. 20.

[340] Cf. pp. 36 f.

[341] Newton, p. 14.

[342] *Ibid.*, p. 61.

[343] *Ibid.*

[344] See Victor Magnien, *Les mystères d'Eleusie* (Paris: 1929), pp. 7–8.

[345] Herrmann, p. 715.

[346] *Ibid.*, p. 717.

[347] "Because my unwitting eyes beheld a crime, I am punished."

[348] Herrmann, pp. 716–717.

[349] *Ibid.*, p. 722.

[350] "I have done naught that the law forbids."

[351] When Baudelaire says, in *Les fleurs du mal* (XCIV)

> Insatiablement avide
> de l'obscur et de l'incertain,
> je ne geindrai pas comme Ovide
> chassé du paradis latin,

he means that he, *unlike* Ovid, is *avide de l'obscur* and would therefore have found so much that was exotic, novel, and mysterious in Tomis that he, unlike Ovid, would not have complained at being deprived of *les paradis artificiels* of Roman society. Of course, as we have already hinted, if Baudelaire meant this seriously, he was mistaken concerning his own character, but that is quite another question.

[352] Samuel B. Platner, and Thomas Ashby, *A Topographical Dictionary of Ancient Rome* (London: Oxford University Press, 1929), p. 85.

[353] Perhaps the greatest secret was the real name of the goddess that was never to be revealed to a male, but Varro and Cornelius Labeo (ap. Mac. *Sat.* I, 12. 21 and 27), apparently independently of one another, knew that it was Fauna.

[354] Clodius, it will be remembered, had to make his escape before the ceremonies were far advanced.

[355] Adolf Greifenhagen, "Bona Dea," *Mitteilungen des deutschen archaeologischen Instituts, Römische Abteilung,* LII (1937), pp. 227–244; cf. W. H. Roscher, *Ausführliches Lexikon der griechischen und*

römischen Mythologie (Leipzig: B. G. Teubner), I, 789 ff.; Wissowa, "Bona Dea," Pauly-Wissowa-Kroll, III¹, pp. 687 ff.

[356] That of Auxesia and Damia, according to Festus, 60. 1 Lindsay, who probably obtained his information from an earlier author.

[357] Juvenal's revelation (VI. 314 ff.) of the *nota Bonae secreta Deae*, aside from his allegation that the ceremonies (in his day) ended in a general debauch, gives us few details, but his assurance that "nil ibi per ludum simulabitur, omnia fient ad verum," will suggest possible rites to anyone who remembers the basic legend that Faunus, having vainly sought to seduce his daughter by giving her wine, assumed the form of a snake and so succeeded in uniting himself to her. The drinking of wine under a pretense that it was milk is one of the best known details of the ceremony, and archaeological evidence shows that the snake was sacred in the cult—see Franz Cumont, "La Bona Dea et ses serpents," *Mélanges d'archéologie et d'histoire* (École Française de Rome), XLIX (1932), pp. 1–5. On the other hand, if the cult was influenced by that of Auxesia and Damia, and these figures were identified with Demeter and Persephone, one may think of Baubo.

[358] T. IV, 4. 25: "vereare . . . ne sim tibi crimen"; cf. IV, 9. 26.

[359] "I have written six books, plus as many more, of a Calendar, and each roll ends together with its own month. This was written not long ago, Caesar, under your own name, but my lot broke off the work that was dedicated to you."

[360] See especially Owen, *TLS, ad loc.,* and the latest edition, *Fastorum Libri VI,* ed. C. Landi et L. Castiglioni, Corpus Scriptorum Latinorum Paravianum (Torino: 1950), pp. vii–xii.

[361] This is the explanation that Owen accepts.

[362] "Even when I was setting forth into exile I burned certain verse that would have found favor." This is Herrmann's explanation: Ovid destroyed the work that was the real cause of his misfortune.

[363] See Landi-Castiglioni, pp. 219 f.

[364] The reference is included among the *dubia* in recent editions of the *fragmenta* of Ovid (19, Owen; 1, Lenz); cf. Landi-Castiglioni, p. x.

[365] It is possible, of course, that the revision, dedicating the work to Germanicus, was begun before the death of Augustus, although a number of passages were written after Ovid heard of that event. For a list of these, see Landi-Castiglioni, p. ix. This possibility, however, would merely make even more extraordinary the conduct on which we here comment.

[366] Cf. Owen, *TLS,* p. 281: "Broken in spirit, he seems to have left his work for some time untouched, which is strange, as nothing might have atoned for the offense of the *Ars amatoria* better than the *Fasti,* a patriotic work which was probably designed, like the early odes of the third book of Horace, to support the religious revival of Augustus." But it is difficult to imagine a spirit too broken to make use of a complete or virtually complete work, and yet not broken enough to prevent com-

position of the *Tristia*—to say nothing of the *Ibis* and perhaps other works.

[367] Owen, *TLS*, p. 85.

[368] Frederick H. Cramer, *Astrology in Roman Law and Politics,* The American Philosophical Society, Memoirs, vol. 37 (Philadelphia: 1954), p. 99.

[369] Salomon Reinach, "Les compagnons et l'exil d'Ovide," *Révue de Philologie de Littérature et d'Histoire Anciennes,* XXXIV (1910), p. 348; Cramer, pp. 102–103.

[370] Cramer, p. 86.

[371] "Made my eyes witness a baleful evil."

[372] Reinach, p. 347.

[373] Herrmann, p. 713.

[374] But he was really in exile because Julius Caesar had not yet pardoned him for his part in the Civil War, and his friend Cicero who had good hopes of procuring his pardon in the autumn of 46 B.C., did not even mention Nigidius' Pythagorean or magic practices, let alone consider them an obstacle to his recall by Caesar (*ad fam.* IV, 13). Nigidius died in the following year—possibly before Cicero had a chance to intercede with Caesar.

[375] The only real evidence that we have for a persecution in this period is the subterranean basilica at Porta Maggiore—if this really was closed as part of a general action against the sect, and if the sect was neo-Pythagorean rather than Orphic.

[376] Jerôme Carcopino, "De la Porta Maggiore a Tomis," *Orpheus,* Anul. I, No. 6 (Noembrie-Decembrie, 1925), pp. 307 ff. If Ovid did attend, it must have been from curiosity, provided that his real opinions are reflected in the constant proviso, *si quid sentiunt Manes,* an attitude that would have hindered him from becoming an adept of any cult that included certainty of personal immortality.

[377] Herrmann, p. 714.

[378] Unless we assume that the scandal had two phases, only one of which was generally known—a possibility that we suggest below, p. 118.

[379] In #8 the woman may be Livilla, in #16, Antonia minor. See above, p. 52.

[380] It is indeed extraordinary that in the *Metamorphoses,* which Ovid was at this time polishing for publication, he should have so completely anticipated his own situation by pointing out (*Meta.* III, 141–142) that Actaeon's *error* was a *Fortunae crimen* which had in it nothing of *scelus.*

[381] "It is hard to write to one who can 'write you off.'" With apologies to Macrobius *Sat.* II, 4. 21, on Licinius Pollio and Augustus.

[382] Italics mine; "Such is your devotion to all of the Iulean name that you are injured too if you think any of them is injured."

BIBLIOGRAPHY

BIBLIOGRAPHY

Alexander, William H. "The Culpa of Ovid," *Classical Journal,* LIII (1958), 319–325.

Anonymous. "Réfutation des conjectures de M. Poinsinet de Sivry, sur la cause de l'exil d'Ovide," in *Journal Encyclopédique,* VII (Octobre, 1773), 134–146.

———. "Addition à la réfutation des conjectures de M. Poinsinet de Sivry, sur la cause de l'exil d'Ovide," in *Journal Encyclopédique,* I (Janvier, 1774), 300–313.

———. "Rassegne," *La Parole del Passato,* 59–60 (1958), 202–204.

———. "Ovide," *Grand Dictionnaire Universel du XIXᵉ Siecle,* XI. Paris: Pierre Larousse, 1865——.

Appel, Ernestus. *Quibus de causis Ovidius ab Augusto relegatus est.* Dissertation, Leipzig. Berolini: Typis G. Hickethier, 1872.

Avery, Maurice W. "Ovid's Apologia," *Classical Journal,* XXXII (1936), 92–102.

Battaglia, Salvatore. "Ovidio," in *Enciclopedia Italiana.* Roma; Rizzoli & Co., 1935–1938. Vol. XXV, pp. 825–829.

Bayeux, *Traduction des Fastes d'Ovide.* Rouen et Paris: 1783–1788. 6 vols.

Bayle, Pierre. "Ovide," in *Dictionnaire Historique et Critique.* 4th ed.; Leiden: Samuel Luchtmans, 1730.

Bickel, Ernst. *Geschichte der römischen Literatur.* Heidelberg: Carl Winter, 1937.

Binsfield, John P. *Observationes Ovidianae Criticae.* Bonn: Carl Georgi, 1860.

Blum, C. "Cur Ovidius relegatus fuerit," *Analele Dobrogei,* Anulele IX, Vol. II (1928).

Boissier, Gaston. "L'Exil d'Ovide," *Revue des Deux Mondes,* LXIX (1867), 580–612.

———. *L'opposition sous les Césars.* Paris: Librairie Hachette et Cⁱᵉ, 1892.

Bradford, Gamaliel. "*Ovid Among the Goths,*" *Yale Review,* IV, 3. (April, 1915), 544–559.

Brooks, Nathan C. *The Metamorphoses of Publius Ovidius Naso.* New York: A. S. Barnes & Co., 1866.

Browne, R. W. *A History of Roman Classical Literature.* London: Richard Bentley, 1853.

Burmannus, Petrus. *Publii Ovidii Nasonis Ibis.* Vol. IV. Amstelodami: Franciscus Changuion, 1727.

———. *P. Ovidii Nasonis Opera.* Oxonii: Talboys et Wheeler, 1825. 2 vols.

Cacciabue, Secundus. *De Ovidii relegationis causis.* Alessandria: G. M. Piccone, 1897.

Carcopino, Jerôme. "Archeologia et Philologie," *Revue des Études Latines,* V (1927), 146–149.

———. "De la Porta Maggiore à Tomis," *Orpheus* (1925), pp. 289–313.

Cartault, Auguste. "Encore les causes de la rélégation d'Ovide," *Mélanges offerts à M. Émile Chatelain.* Paris: Librairie Ancienne, Honoré Champion, 1910.

Catrou, F. et P. J. Rouillé, *Histoire Romaine.* Paris: Rollin, 1725–1737. 20 vols.

Cary, M. *A History of Rome.* London: Macmillan & Co., Ltd., 1954.

[Celsanus, Barnabas]. *Publius Ovidius Naso.* Venitiis, Bernardinus Rizus, 1486–1487. General editor's name, Barnabas Celsanus, suppressed. This work is a reprint of edition published by H. Liechtenstein, Vicenza, 1480, but with suppression of Celsanus' name.

———. *Ovidius Naso, P. Opera.* Vicentiae: Hermannus Liechtenstein, 1480.

Charpentier, J. P. "Sur Ovide," in *Oeuvres complètes d'Ovide.* Vol. I, Bibliothèque latine-française. Paris: C. L. F. Pankoucke, 1834.

Church, Alfred. *Ovid.* Philadelphia: J. B. Lippincott Co., 1876.

Cnipping, Borchard. *P. Ovidii Nasonis Operum, Tomus I, II, III.* Lugduni Batavorum, ex officina Hackiana, 1670. 3 vols.

Cocchia, Enrico. "La relegazione di Ovidio a Tomi," *Atti della Reale Academia di Archeologia, Lettere e Belle Arti,* XXII (1902), 1–145.

Coon, Raymond H. "Ovid in Exile," *Classical Journal,* XXII (1927), 355–369.

Cooper, Clyde B. *Some Elizabethan Opinions of the Poetry and Character of Ovid.* Dissertation, University of Chicago. Menasha, Wis.: The Collegiate Press, 1914.

Cramer, Frederick H. *Astrology in Roman Law and Politics.* The American Philosophical Society, Memoirs, vol. 37. Philadelphia: 1954.

Crusius, O. "Entstehungszeit und Verfasser von Ps.-Apuleius De Orthographia," *Philologus,* XLVII (1889), 434–448.

Cruttwell, Charles T. *A History of Roman Literature.* New York: Charles Scribner's Sons, 1877.

Cumont, Franz. "La Bona Dea et ses serpents," *Mélanges d'Archéologie et d'Histoire* (École Française de Rome), XLIX (1932), 1–5.

———. *The Oriental Religions in Roman Paganism.* New York: Dover Publications, Inc., 1956.

———. *Astrology and Religion.* New York: Dover Publications, Inc., 1960.

D'Elia, Salvatore. "L'esilio di Ovidio e alcuni aspetti della storia augustea," *Annali della facolta di lettere e di filosofia,* Università de Napoli, V (1955), 95–157.

Dessau, Hermann. *Geschichte der römischen Kaiserzeit.* Berlin: Weidmannsche Buchhandlung, 1924. 2 vols.

———. *Prosopographia Imperii Romani.* Berlin: George Reimer, 1897. 3 vols.

Deville, A. *Essai sur l'exil d'Ovide.* Paris: Firmin Didot Frères, Fils et Cᵗᵉ, 1859.

Durling, Robert M. "Ovid as *Praeceptor Amoris*," *Classical Journal,* LIII (1958), 157–167.

Dyer, Thomas. "On the Cause of Ovid's Exile," *The Classical Museum,* IV (1847), 229–247.

———. "Ovid," in *A Dictionary of Greek and Roman Biography and Mythology,* ed. Sir William Smith. London: John Murray, 1890. 3 vols.

Ehwald, Rudolph. *Ad historiam carminum Ovidianorum recensionemque symbolae,* III. Gotha: Engelhard-Reyherschen, 1892.

———, "Jahresbericht über Ovid vom Juli 1886 bis Dezember 1893," *Jahresbericht über die Fortschritte der classischen Altertumswissenschaft,* LXXX (1895), 1–118.

———. "Jahresbericht über Ovid vom Mai 1894 bis Januar 1902," *Jahresbericht über die Fortschritte der classischen Altertumswissenschaft,* CIX (1902), 162–302.

Ellis, R. *P. Ovidii Nasonis Ibis.* Oxonii: e typographeo Clarendoniano, 1881.

Fabricius, Johann Albert. *Bibliotheca Latina.* Hamburgi: sumtu Viduae Benjamini Schilleri & Jo. Christoph. Kisneri, 1721.

Fargues, Pierre. "Ovide, l'homme et le poète," *Revue des Cours et Conférences,* Iʳᵉ Serie, XLI (1939), 205–212.

Federico, Ermolao. *Discorsi sopra la vita di P. Ovidio Nasone.* Venezia: Giuseppe Antonelli, 1844–1848.

Fleury-Cuvillier, A. A. "Ovide," *Revue de Paris,* XVI (1830), 200–216.

Fournier-Pescay. "Ovidio," *Biografia Universale* (Venezia), XLII (1828), 122–151.

Fränkel, Hermann. *Ovid: A Poet Between Two Worlds.* Berkeley and Los Angeles: University of California Press, 1945.

Funck, John Nicolas. *De Virili aetate latinae linguae tractatus.* Marburi Cattorum: ex officina Philippi Casimiri Mulleri, 1727.

Garlow, Lou W. "A Guess As to Why Ovid Was Exiled," *Classical Journal*, XXXII (1936), 103–105.

Ginguené, P. L. "Les Metamorphoses d'Ovide," *Mercure de France*, XXXVIII (1809), 28–40.

———. "Extrait d'une dissertation italienne sur l'exil d'Ovide," *La Decade Philosophique Littéraire et Politique*, vol. 2 no. 15 (An IX 2me trimestre), pp. 336–351.

Goujet, Pierre Claude, Abbé. "Ovide," in *Bibliothèque Françoise*, vol. 6. 2d ed.; Paris: Mariette & Guerin, 1747.

Graeber, Gustav, *Untersuchungen über Ovids Briefe aus der Verbannung*. Elberfeld: Gedruckt bei Sam. Lucas, 1884.

Greifenhagen, Adolf. "Bona Dea," *Mitteilungen des deutschen archeologischen Instituts*, Römische Abteilung, LII (1937), 227–244.

Groag, Edmundus and Stein, Arturus. *Prosographia Imperii Romani*. Berlin: Walter de Gruyter & Co., 1933———.

Haight, E. H. *Italy Old & New*. New York: E. P. Dutton & Co., 1922.

Hammond, Mason. "Plato and Ovid's Exile," *Harvard Studies in Classical Philology*, LXIII (1958), 347–361.

d'Hancarville, Pierre Francois Hugues. *Monumens de la vie privée des douze Césars*. À Caprées, chez Sebellius, 1782.

Hardy, E. G. (ed.). *C. Plinii Caecilii Secundi epistulae ad Traianum Imperatorem cum eiusdem responsis*. London: Macmillan & Co., 1889.

Hartmann, J. J. "De Ovidio poeta commentatio," *Mnemosyne*, XXXIII (1905), 99–124.

———. *De Ovidio poeta*. Lugduni Batavorum: E. J. Brill, 1905.

Heinsius, Daniel (ed.). *Pub. Ovidii Nasonis Opera*. Lugduni Batavorum: ex officina Elzeviriana, 1629.

Heitler, Moriz. *Ovids Verbannung*. Wien: Moritz Perles, 1898.

Herrmann, Léon. "La faute secrète d'Ovide," *Revue Belge de Philologie et d'Histoire*, XVII (1938), 695–725.

Highet, Gilbert. *The Classical Tradition*. New York: Oxford University Press, 1957.

Horváth, I. K. "Impius Aeneas," *Acta Antiqua Academiae Scientiarum Hungaricae*, VI (1958), 385–393.

Huber, Johann. *Die Ursachen der Verbannung des Ovid*. Stadtamhof: J. K. Mayr, 1887–1888.

Huygens, R. B. C. "Accessus ad Auctores," in *Collection Latomus*, 15 (Bruxelles: 1954), 1–48.

Jones, A. H. M. *Studies in Roman Government and Law*. New York: Frederick A. Praeger, Inc., 1960.

de Jonghe, Theodore J. *Publii Ovidii Nasonis Tristium Liber IV*. Groningen: de Waal, 1945.

Klotz, Alfred. *Geschichte der römischen Literatur*. Leipzig: Velhagen & Klazing, 1930.

Koerber, E. *De P. Ovidii Nasonis relegationis caussis commentatio.* St. Petersburg: E. Weinecke, 1883.

Kraemer, A. Review of "The Second Book of Ovid's *Tristia*," a lecture by Robinson Ellis, in *Wochenschrift für klassische Philologie,* XXXI (1914), 874–875.

Kraus, Walter. "Der Forschungsbericht, Ovid," I. Bericht, 1 Teil, *Anzeiger für die Altertumswissenschaft,* XI (1958), 129–146.

La Penna, Antonio. *Ibis.* Biblioteca di studi superiori, Vol. XXXIV. Firenze: 1957.

———. *Scholia in P. Ovidi Nasonis Ibin.* Biblioteca di studi superiori, Vol. XXXV. Firenze: 1959.

Lehman, Paul. *Pseudo-Antike Literatur des Mittelalters.* Studien der Bibliothek Warburg, vol. 13. Leipzig: B. G. Teubner, 1927.

Lenz, Friedrich. "Ovid. Bericht über das Schrifttum der Jahre 1928–1937," *Jahresbericht über die Fortschritte der classischen Altertumswissenschaft,* CCXLIV (1939), 1–168.

Leopold, H. M. R. *Exulum Trias.* Goudae: Koch et Knuttel, 1904.

Lepore, Ettore. "Da Cicerone a Ovidio," *La Parola del Passato,* 59–60 (1958), 81–130.

Levy, Friedrich. Review of "P. Ovidi Nasonis Tristium Liber Secundus," by S. G. Owen, *Gnomon,* II (1926), 263–274.

Leutsch, E. L. "Ovidius," *Allgemeine Encyklopädie der Wissenschaften und Kunste,* vol. 8. Leipzig: Dritte Sektion, 1836.

Magnus, Hugo. "Commentarius exegeticus ad Ovidii Tristia" (Budapest: 1913); and "Commentarius exegeticus ad Ovidii Epistulas ex Ponto" (Budapest: 1915), *Berliner Philologische Wochenschrift,* VII (1920), 153–160.

Maidment, James, and William H. Logan (eds.). *The Dramatic Works of Sir Aston Cokayne.* Edinburgh: W. Paterson, 1874.

Marache, R. "La Révolte d'Ovide exilé contre Auguste," *Ovidiana, Recherches sur Ovide,* ed. N. I. Herescu, Paris, Société d'Edition "Les Belles Lettres" (1958), pp. 412–419.

Marin, Demetrio. "Intorno alle cause dell' esilio di Ovidio," *Ovidiana, Recherches sur Ovide,* ed. N. I. Herescu, Paris, Société d'Edition "Les Belles Lettres" (1958), pp. 406–411.

———. "Ovidio fu relegato per la sua opposizione al regime Augusteo?" *Fasti Pontici Ovidio poetae dicati = Acta Philologica* (Acad. Dacoromana), I (1958), 97 ff.

Marinescu, I. M. "De ce a Fost Exilat Ovidiu?" *Publius Ovidius Naso,* Biblioteca Antica Studii, II, Editura Academiei Republicii Populare Romine (1957), 101–118.

Magnien, Victor. *Les mystères d'Eleusis.* Paris: 1929.

Marót, Karoly. "L'esilio di Ovidio," *Acta Antiqua Academiae Scientiarum Hungaricae,* III (1955), 223–232.

Martinelli, Nelli. "Carmen et Error," *Carmina Certaminis Poetici Hoeuff-*

tiani. Amstelodami: Academia Disciplinarum Nederlandica, 1953. Pp. 5–38.

Martini, E., *Einleitung zu Ovid.* Brünn: Rohrer, 1933.

Masefield, John. *A Letter from Pontus.* New York: Macmillan Co., 1936.

Masera, Giovanni. *Ovidi Tristium Lib. II.* Turin: 1929.

Masson, Joannes. *P. Ovidii Nasonis Vita.* Amstelodami: apud viduam Joannis Janssonii a Waesberge, 1708.

Meiser, Karl. "Über Ovids Begnadigungsgesuch," *Sitzungsberichte der philosophisch-philologischen und der historischen Klasse der K. B. Academie der Wissenschaften zu München* (1907), pp. 171–205.

Merkelius, Rudolphus. *P. Ovidii Nasonis Tristium Libri Quinque et Ibis.* Berolini: Sumptibus G. Reimeri, 1837.

Milton, John. *Areopagitica.* London: Alex. Murray & Son, 1868.

Minich, S. R. "Sulle cagione della relegazione d'Ovidio a Tomi," *Atti del Reale Istituto Veneto di Scienze, Lettere, ed Arti,* Serie quinta, VI (1879–1880), 1131–1174.

de Mirmont, H. de La Ville. *La jeunesse d'Ovide.* Paris: Albert Fontemoing, 1905.

Moehring, Horst R. "The Persecution of the Jews and the Adherents of the Isis Cult at Rome," *Novum Testamentum,* III (1959), 293 ff.

Mohr, Paul. *Sidonius.* Leipzig: B. G. Teubner, 1895.

Mommsen, Theodor. *Römisches Staatsrecht.* Leipzig: verlag von S. Hirzel, 1874.

———. *Römisches Strafrecht.* Leipzig: verlag von Duncker & Humblot, 1899.

Mozley, J. H. *Ovid: The Art of Love and Other Poems.* Cambridge, Mass.: Harvard University Press, 1957.

Müldener. "Zu Ovid," *Philologus,* IX (1854), 577–579.

Munk, Eduard. *Geschichte der classischen Literatur der Römer.* Berlin: Ferd. Dummler, 1859. 2 vols.

Munro, H. A. J. *Criticisms and Elucidations of Catullus,* Cambridge: Deighton, Bell Co., 1878.

Mylonas, George E., *Eleusis and the Eleusinian Mysteries.* Princeton: Princeton University Press, 1961.

Nageotte, Eugène, *Ovide, sa vie, ses oeuvres.* Dissertation, Dijon. Mâcon: Émile Protat, 1872.

Némethy, Geyza. *Supplementum Commentariorum ad Ovidii Amores, Tristia et Epistulas ex Ponto.* Budapestini: sumptibus Academiae Litterarum Hungaricae, 1922.

———. *Commentarius Exegeticus Ad Ovidii Tristia.* Budapestini: sumptibus Academiae Litterarum Hungaricae, 1913.

Newton, John Henry. *Three Enigmas.* London: Thomas Hookham, 1821.

Niedermeier, Lorenz. *Untersuchungen über die antike poetische Autobiographie.* München: Dr. C. Wolf & Sohn, 1919.

Nisard, M. *Ovide, Oeuvres complètes.* Collection des Auteurs Latins. Paris: Firmin Didot Frères, 1850.

Nogara, B. "Di alcune vite e commenti medioevali di Ovidio," *Miscellanea Ceriani.* Milano: Ulrico Hoepli, 1910, 413–431.

Norwood, Frances. "The Riddle of Ovid's 'Relegatio,' " *Classical Philology,* LVIII (1963), 150–163.

Oliver, Revilo P. "The First Edition of the Amores," *Transactions of the American Philological Association,* LXXVI (1945), 191–215.

————. " 'New Fragments' of Latin Authors in Perotti's Cornucopiae," *Transactions of the American Philological Association,* LXXVIII (1947), 376–424.

O'Neil, Edward N. "Cynthia and the Moon," *Classical Philology,* LIII (1958), 1 ff.

L'Orange, H. P. "Das Geburtsritual der Pharaonen am römischen Kaiserhof," *Symbolae Osloenses,* XXI (1941), 105–116.

Otis, Brooks. "Ovid and the Augustans," *Transactions and Proceedings of the American Philological Association,* LXIX (1938), 188–229.

Ouwens, R., *Noctes Haganae.* Frankfurt: 1780.

Publii Ovidii Nasonis Sulmonensis Poetae Operum Tomus Primus, Secundus, Tertius. Francofurti: typis Wechelianis apud Claudium Marnium & heredes Ioannis Aubrij, 1601. 3 vols.

Owen, S. G. Review of "Die Ursachen der Verbannung des Ovid," by J. Huber, *Classical Review,* III (1889), 311.

————. *P. Ovidi Nasonis Tristium Libri V.* Oxonii: e Typographeo Clarendoniano, 1889.

————. "Ovid," in *The Encyclopaedia Britannica.* Vol. XX 11th ed.; Cambridge, England: University Press, 1910–1911.

————. *Tristium Liber Secundus.* Oxford: Clarendon Press, 1924.

————, in collaboration with anonymous author. "Ovid," in *The Encyclopaedia Britannica,* Vol. XVI. Chicago: 1942.

————. "Ovid," *The Oxford Classical Dictionary,* Oxford: Clarendon Press, 1949.

Palmer, Arthur (ed.). *P. Ovidi Nasonis Heroides.* Oxford: Clarendon Press, 1898.

Pansa, Giovanni. *Ovidio.* Sulmona: Angeletti, 1924.

Paratore, Ettore. Review of "Il tempo di Augusto," by Mario A. Levi, *Maia,* V (1952), 145–160.

————. *Storia della letteratura latina.* Firenze: G. C. Sansoni, 1951.

Perotti, Nicolai. *Cornucopiae.* Basileae: apud Valentinum Curionem, 1526.

Peter, Hermann. *P. Ovidi Nasonis Fastorum Libri Sex.* Leipzig and Berlin: B. G. Teubner, 1907.

Pichon, R. "Ovide," in *La Grande Encyclopédie.* Vol. XXV. Paris: E. Arrault et C¹ᵉ, n.d.

Platner, Samuel B., and Thomas Ashby. *A Topographical Dictionary of Ancient Rome.* London: Oxford University Press, 1929.

Plessis, Frédéric. *La Poésie latine.* Paris: Librairie C. Klincksieck, 1909.

Pohlenz, Max. "Die Abfassungszeit von Ovids Metamorphosen," *Hermes,* XLVIII (1913), 1–13.

Pokrowskij, Michael. "Neue Beiträge zur Charakteristik Ovids," *Philologus,* Supplementband XI (1907–1910), 351–404.

Polenton, Sicco. *Scriptorum Illustrium Latinae Linguae Libri XVIII,* ed. B. L. Ullman (American Academy in Rome, Papers, vol. 6). Rome: 1928.

Przychocki, Gustav. "De Ovidii 'Caesarea Puella,'" *Wiener Studien,* XXXVI (1915), 340–342.

Rand, Edward Kennard. *Ovid & His Influence.* New York: Longmans, Green & Co., 1928.

Reinach, Salomon. "Le tombeau d'Ovide," *Revue de Philologie,* XXX (1906), 275–285.

———. "Les compagnons et l'exil d'Ovide," *Revue de Philologie de Littérature et d'Histoire Anciennes,* XXXIV (1910), 342–349.

———. *Cultes, mythes et religions.* Paris: Ernest Leroux, 1912.

Ribbeck, Otto. *Geschichte der römischen Dichtung.* Stuttgart: J. G. Cotta'sche Buchhandlung Nachfolger, 1900.

Riccardi, G. *Brevi osservazione sulla relegazione di Ovidio.* Palermo: 1896.

Riese, Alexander. "Jahresbericht über die Litteratur zu Ovid aus den Jahren 1880 und 1881," *Jahresbericht über die Fortschritte der classischen Altertumswissenschaft,* XXVII (1883), 72–92.

Riley, Henry T. *The Fasti, Tristia, Pontic Epistles, Ibis, and Halieuticon of Ovid.* London: George Bell & Sons, 1890.

Ripert, Émile. *Ovide, poète de l'amour, des dieux et de l'exil.* Paris: Librairie Armand Colin, 1921.

Rochefort, Ribault de, M. "L'exil d'Ovide, Dissertation," *Journal des Sçavans,* CXXX (1743), 254–263.

Rosa, Lucia. "Due biografie medievali di Ovidio," *La Parola del Passato,* 59–60 (1958), 168–172.

Roscher, W. H. *Ausführliches Lexikon der griechischen und römischen Mythologie.* Leipzig: B. G. Teubner, 1884–1937. 6 vols.

Rose, H. J. *A Handbook of Latin Literature.* New York: E. P. Dutton & Co., 1936.

Rosmini, Carlo. *Vita d'Ovidio Nasone.* Milan: Giuseppe Pogliani, 1821.

Rostagni, Augusto. *Ibis.* Contributi alla Scienza dell' Antichita, Vol. III. Firenze: Felice Le Monnier, 1920.

Roth, C. L. "Beitrag zur Lösung eines alten Rathsels," *Correspondenz = Blatt für die Gelehrten-und Real-Schulen Württembergs,* I (1854), 185–187.

Schanz, Martin, and Carl Hosius. *Geschichte der römischen Literatur.* Müller's Handbuch der Altertumswissenschaft, Vol. VIII. München: C. H. Beck'sche Verlagsbuchhandlung, 1935. 2 vols.

Schoell, M. S. F. *Histoire abrégée de la littérature romaine.* Paris: 1815. 4 vols.

Schmidt, Wilhelm Adolf. *Geschichte der Denk-und glaubensfreiheit.* Berlin: Verlag von Veit und Comp., 1847.

Schoemann, Georg. "Eine Muthmassung über den wahren Grund von Ovids Relegation," *Philologus,* XLI (1882), 171–175.

Sedlmayer, H. S. "Beiträge zur Geschichte der Ovidstudien im Mittelalter," *Wiener Studien,* VI (1884), 142–158.

Seeck, O. "Zur Geschichte des Isiskultus in Rom," *Hermes,* XLIII (1908), 642 ff.

Sellar, W. Y. "Ovid," in *The Encyclopaedia Britannica.* Vol. XVIII. 9th ed.; London: 1885.

———. *The Roman Poets of the Augustan Age.* Oxford: Clarendon Press, 1899.

Siegmund, A. "Seneca und Ovidius," *Wiener Studien,* XXI (1899), 156–157.

Simcox, George A. *A History of Latin Literature.* New York: Harper & Bros., 1883. 2 vols.

de Sivry, Poinsinet. "Lettre . . . sur la vraie cause de l'exil d'Ovide," *Mercure de France,* I (Avril, 1773), 181–185.

Smith, Kirby Flower. *Martial, the Epigrammatist.* Baltimore: Johns Hopkins Press, 1920.

Strachan-Davidson, James Leigh. *Problems of the Roman Criminal Law.* Oxford: Clarendon Press, 1912. 2 vols.

Teuffel, Wilhelm S. *History of Roman Literature.* Revised & enlarged by Ludwig Schwabe; transl. by George C. Warr. London: George Bell & Sons, 1891. 2 vols.

Thomas, Émile. "Sur les causes de l'exil d'Ovide," *Revue de Philologie de Littérature et d'Histoire Anciennes,* XIII (1889), 47–50.

Tiraboschi, Girolamo. *Storia della letteratura italiana.* Milano: Nicolo Bettoni e Comp., 1833. 3 vols.

Trozzi, Mario. *Ovidio e i suoi tempi.* Catania: Vincenzo Muglia, 1930.

Vannuci, Atto. *Studi storici e morali sulla letteratura latina.* 3d ed.; Torino: Ermanno Loescher, 1886.

Villenave, G. T. "Ovide," in *Biographie Universelle Ancienne et Moderne.* Vol. XXXI. Paris: Michaud, 1805.

Voltaire, F. M. A. *Questions sur l'Encyclopédie.* Vol. II. Paris: 1770.

———. *Dictionnaire Philosophique.* Paris: Armand-Aubree, 1829. Vol. II.

Wilkinson, L. P. *Ovid Recalled.* Cambridge: Cambridge University Press, 1955.

172   BIBLIOGRAPHY

Winther, H. Review of Giuseppe Riccardi's "Brevi osservazione sulla
     relegazione di Ovidio," *Wochenschrift für klassische Philologie,*
     XIV (1897), 871.
Wissowa, G. "Ovidius Naso," in *Real-Encyclopädie der classischen Alter-
     tumswissenschaft,* Ed. Pauly-Wissowa-Kroll. Stuttgart: J. B. Metz-
     lersche Verlagsbuchhandlung, 1942.
————. *Religion und Kultus der Römer.* München: 1902.
Withof, Johann H. *Kritische Anmerkungen.* Düsseldorf: Johann Christ,
     Danzer, 1791. 2 vols.
Wright, F. A. *The Lover's Handbook.* New York: E. P. Dutton, 192–.
————. *Three Roman Poets.* New York: E. P. Dutton & Co., 1938.
Zingerle, Anton. *Martial's Ovid Studien.* Innsbruck: Verlag der Wagner'-
     schen Universitäts-Buchhandlung, 1877.
Zimmermann, Rudolph. "Die Ursachen von Ovids Verbannung," *Rhein-
     isches Museum für Philologie,* LXXXI (1932), 263–274.

INDEX

INDEX